Training Design and Delivery
Second Edition

Geri E. McArdle

Alexandria, VA

ASTD Press is an internationally renowned source of insightful and practical information on workplace learning and performance topics, including training basics, evaluation and return-on-investment (ROI), instructional systems development (ISD), e-learning, leadership, and career development.

Ordering information: Books published by ASTD Press can be purchased by visiting our website at store.astd.org or by calling 800.628.2783 or 703.683.8100.

Library of Congress Control Number: 2006937422

ISBN-10: 1-56286-470-X
ISBN-13: 978-1-56286-470-5

ASTD Press Editorial Staff
Director: Cat Russo
Manager, Acquisitions & Author Relations: Mark Morrow
Editorial Manager: Jacqueline Edlund-Braun
Editorial Assistant: Maureen Soyars
Retail Trade Specialist: Nancy Silva

Copyeditors: April Michelle Davis, Ann Lee Bruen
Proofreader: Kris Patenaude
Interior Design and Production: Kathleen Schaner
Cover Design: Kristi Sone
Cover Illustration: Image Zoo

Printed by Victor Graphics, Inc., Baltimore, Maryland, www.victorgraphics.com.

Contents

Preface

Management offers education and professional development training, hoping to increase personal and workplace satisfaction, motivation, and productivity, but the return-on-investment is realized only if training programs, both informal and formal, are well defined, delivered, and evaluated.

Training Design and Delivery provides a comprehensive resource for training managers and trainers who are responsible for the planning, organization, design, implementation, and evaluation of training programs.

The first part of the book provides basic training design strategies that will enhance presentations and capture a learner's attention to participate in the learning process. Specific strategies include ways to create trainings that guarantee successful training transfer of concepts on the job, detailed descriptions of how learning occurs and how to manage the training-learning interactions with ease, and ways to establish trainer and presentation credibility early in a training presentation.

The second part of the book presents an easy-to-use recipe for designing and developing training—a training systems development model. This training systems development model is a theoretical model that establishes the building blocks to use when organizing your training topics. This multistep training systems development model presents a 20-step process for analyzing, designing, developing, implementing, and evaluating trainings.

The third part of the book includes a trainer's tool kit, which provides answers to the major problem areas encountered during design and implementation. The tool kit has two sections. The first describes the technique, and the second, the application of each technique.

Training Design and Delivery is applicable to training in almost every sector: commercial, industrial, as well as educational in both the public and private sectors.

Preface

I wrote this book with myself in mind. When I began my career as a trainer and human resource manager, I couldn't find a simple book that described the steps to use in developing and implementing training. I promised myself that once I'd mastered the process, I would share it with others so they wouldn't have the fear of the unknown that I had without a road map.

Geri E. McArdle
August 2007

Introduction

These are exciting times. With advances in computer technology, we're all witnessing a revitalized effort in the fields of knowledge engineering, expert systems, and multimedia educational technology. For many people, these emerging technologies are tools in training design and delivery systems, as well as in the way we study learning and conceive the learning process.

My own discovery of the instructional systems development model in the training industry and the current movement toward performance systems technology have an effect on my role as a trainer and an instructional designer. Training must consist of a well-planned, organized learning event that can ensure an outcome for the learner and the sponsoring organization. I'm sure you, too, have encountered or are starting to encounter ripples from these trends in designing and delivering training that provide a return on both investment training dollars and the use of cutting-edge technologies and training tools.

Training Basics

Learning is all about helping people to develop as individuals and career professionals. The core to this development is training. Training can increase individual competence, as well as open doors for future opportunities. The first part of this book presents a review of the tools, techniques, and strategies that trainers and instructional designers use to develop basic training content.

Over the past two decades, the training field has been one of the more rapidly growing business sectors in the U.S. economy. This growth is in response to the rapid expansion of the global marketplace, the increase in diversity of workers, and the global demand for a skilled workforce. Further, the knowledge and skills gained by workers just a decade ago are, in some cases, no longer sufficient to equip a person for a lifetime of work.

As organizations grow, learn, and change, training must evolve. Finding, and especially retaining, qualified candidates to meet long-term organizational needs is becoming critical to corporate success. As a result, organizations are no longer just providing job-specific, technical skills; rather, they are focusing more on training that develops the entire person. Such offerings (managing stress, team building, dealing with difficult people, analyzing personal styles, solving problems creatively, and building consensus and sensitivity to diversity) are becoming part of the standard corporate curriculum. By encouraging employees to learn more about themselves and their capabilities, and to take responsibility for their own learning, organizations are banking talent for future use.

As trainers, we need to enhance our skills so we are able to motivate participants to learn more about themselves and their capabilities as they relate to the organization and to create a desire for self-directed learning. The need to provide training in a variety of venues is becoming increasingly important. The trainer who understands and can design and use e-learning, distance learning, blended learning, and self-study along with traditional learning is in high demand.

Now is the time to develop a new training system—one that equips individuals to cope with this change. We should be moving away from the traditional method of transmitting knowledge and toward helping people to view learning as a lifelong activity. As trainers and instructional developers, we should change the delivery emphasis of *what* knowledge or skill we affect to *how* we help people to learn and ask questions to help them acquire skills of self-directed inquiry.

Training Design

No matter how high-tech or low-tech trainers and their training designs may be, the designs will have to adhere to the demanding standards of training design. No training is successful unless the instructional design meets these standards of quality, and the quality of design, development, and delivery has its basis in a scientific approach in the area of human learning.

The multistep training program design tool, in the second part of this book, is an easy-to-use guide for designing and developing a training module and program, whether it will be a computerized program or a low-tech, in-house workshop. The steps take trainers from responding to the initial training request to delivering and evaluating the training program. Specifically created for this book, the training program design tool sets forth a number of critical elements. Although hundreds of training practitioners use the critical elements in this training program design tool when they design and develop training programs, the training program design tool organizes the steps and begins with a little-used step: business justification. This first step leads management to buy in to the training, which is essential for successful training. By following the training program design tool, trainers will be on the road to providing successful trainings.

The third part of this book presents success tools and techniques that you can use to open a training, conduct a review, and close with a bang.

Enjoy the training journey that this book provides as a source in your everyday practice.

▼ Part I

Training Basics

Training Overview

As we have become used to the way technology and business demands have changed the way we work, our expectations about training have shifted. Organizations and learners have higher expectations than in the past for trainings in the workplace. All training is intended to help individuals gain new and improved knowledge and skills for a specific purpose—to help them learn to do or think about something in a different way. It's all about changing behavior and acquiring new skills for new challenges.

Frequently, an organization conducts training to implement a new program or change a process. Training is often distinguished from education in that training prepares a person to perform a task, improve a behavior, or learn a skill. Education, in contrast, is seen as improving the whole person, preparing the person for life. In today's business world, what we call training can address the goals of education also. Although there are a variety of specific training programs that can be designed or delivered, there are six types of training initiatives that are commonly offered to individuals in organizations. Each type of training initiative targets a certain training need.

1. Training increases individual knowledge and skill.
2. Career development helps individuals assess their strengths, weaknesses, interests, and values, enabling them to explore and select a work path.
3. Team development helps team members work and interact more effectively and efficiently.
4. Organizational development increases organizational capability.

5. Human resource development combines training, career, team, and organizational development to increase workplace health and performance.
6. Performance improvement uses a variety of strategies and tools to increase performance of individuals, groups, processes, and organizations.

This list is a training menu of design and delivery formats. The training format that trainers choose for their design and delivery will depend on the needs of their sponsors, the specific organization, and individual employees.

Changes in Training Design and Delivery

The need for training has always been present in every walk of life, but today the need is much greater. What was appropriate last year as an instructional strategy or a training design might not be appropriate for today's learner. Rapid changes in what constitutes business, and how it is conducted, have rippled in every sector of society and especially in the design and delivery of training.

In the field of training and instructional design, there are four areas that constantly change: course materials, course methods, trainer styles, and learner expectations.

Course Materials

Learners demand easy-to-use materials, with content that focuses on direct application to the job. Also, the design and presentation of the content should include graphics, job aids, and take-homes for future reference.

Course Methods

Learners want clear and easy-to-follow instructional methods that are interactive and have a direct transfer back to the job. The key to using any instructional strategy is to provide an opportunity for the learners to effectively master the content. The principles of learning should be integrated in the course instructional strategy. The specific learning principles that trainers should use in their course design and delivery are

- ▼ involving the learners
- ▼ focusing on the task
- ▼ applying the collaborative approach
- ▼ using a structured design.

Trainer Styles

Learners expect the trainer to be credible and to know the topic. Also, the trainer should be practical and sensitive to all learning styles. The trainer is encouraged to know when to play the role of instructor, coach, facilitator, or consultant.

Learner Expectations

Learners expect to take responsibility for their own learning. They expect to learn from others involved in the instruction process and demand that the content be presented in a manner that promotes successful skill transfer back on the job. Learners also want to be partners in the learning process and be given the opportunity during the session to practice their own facilitating and coaching skills with others.

Given this list of changing expectations, successful trainers must think about how to prepare a training session, how to anticipate outcomes, and how to measure training success.

When trainers think of training, they usually think simply about who is conducting the training and who is going to attend. Yet, there are four key stakeholders who contribute to the success of a training: learner, course designer, course instructor, and learner's employer. Table 2-1 gives an overview of these stakeholders and what they bring to the success of the training.

The training event is an open dialogue, a conversation, and an opportunity to exchange information and ideas. The learning outcome of a training event is the communication that takes place between the learner and the trainer. It should provide the learner with the ability to internalize the information and apply it.

Table 2-1. Key Stakeholders and Their Roles in Successful Training.

Learners Must Ensure That	Course Designers Must Ensure That	Course Instructors Must Ensure That	Employers Must Manage Training to Ensure That
• They will actively work to transfer learning to the job. • They will strive to understand the topic. • They will trust themselves enough to try something new. • They will try to work well in teams.	• Written objectives can be accomplished. • Activities are appropriate for topics. • Course content flow is correct. • Clear directions are given. • Topics are organized logically.	• Materials are easy to implement. • Reference materials are useful. • Learners see the relevance of the topic. • Activities are easily transferred to the job.	• The investment increases the productivity of employees, results in a positive return-on-investment, and is part of the company strategy. • The training connects to the professional growth of the learner and creates more loyal, satisfied employees.

Learning Variables

When trainers plan their training design or delivery, they need to focus on achieving learning outcomes. Trainers need to be sensitive to learner styles, develop instructional strategies that appeal to the learner style needs, and focus on the appropriate level of evaluation to measure the learning. By focusing on all these elements, trainers will automatically integrate opportunities for successful training transfer.

There is no one comprehensive style theory that all educators, researchers, or trainers agree upon; however, they do agree that individuals learn differently. Trainers know that learning is a process that typically begins with observations or reflections by the learners. Once learners become aware of the learning taking place, they build an intellectual data file to store this information.

Gathering information about an audience is a critical step in the development of an effective training program. The key to activating a positive learning situation is to appeal to all the learning styles, be sensitive to what motivates, and use appropriate facilitation skills for all learners.

Appeal to All Learning Styles

Because there are three learning styles—visual, auditory, and kinesthetic—trainers must use a variety of delivery approaches in presenting training events. For example, presentations are effective with visual learners, mini lectures appeal to auditory learners, and hands-on exercises are important for kinesthetic learners.

Motivate the Learners

Adults attend trainings, in most cases, because they want to learn information and skills that help them to do a better job. Providing opportunities for learners to interact with others through in-group discussions, group activities, and thought-provoking questions can enhance a two-way, didactic learning process.

Facilitate for Success

Learners are diverse and come to trainings with different life and educational experiences and different expectations about their work and their lives. These learning differences are based on their backgrounds and characteristics, such as gender, age, life stage, culture, and disability. The learning climate that trainers establish should include the physical surroundings, other people in the room, and intangible elements, such as a relaxed, comfortable atmosphere which permits the learners to feel that they have a degree of control and can ask questions, affect pace, and learn from others. Also, trainers should enable and encourage learners to work together to solve problems. Finally, trainers must use good questioning techniques and encourage learners to ask questions when they are confused. Good questions help to stimulate insight and understanding by encouraging time for inquiry and reflection. Remember, when learners ask questions, trainers can observe where they may be having difficulty.

Training Types

Learning is ultimately the responsibility of the learners: The more learners put into the learning experience, the more they tend to get out of the event. Therefore, the type of training they choose becomes our important issue. A wide range of learning opportunities is available, which can be consolidated and integrated into several types of delivery formats.

Classroom Learning

Classroom learning can vary greatly in approach from the traditional method in which the trainer adopts the role of lecturer, with little or no student participation, to where the trainer adopts the role of facilitator, with the style ranging from nondirective to directive.

Outdoor Learning

Outdoor learning has been widely used for a number of years, mostly by the armed forces, particularly in such fields as leadership training and team building. Some training professionals might argue that this format lacks the academic rigor of classroom instruction, but it is linked with classroom input and debriefing.

Computer-Assisted Learning

Computer-assisted learning is largely a refinement of programmed learning in which individuals work through written material in a programmed way. Learners progress in a step-by-step fashion, having received feedback on their responses. Such programmed learning has become more sophisticated in recent years with the advent of computers, videos, and the Internet. One of the advantages of such training is flexibility. Learners can progress at their own pace. The disadvantage is isolation, which can result in low motivation and reduced commitment and cost.

Simulation Learning

Simulation is participative and used mainly for skills training. It can reinforce other types of training. As far as possible, simulation training is linked to the real world.

Training Methods

There are two categories of training:

1. trainer-centered
2. learner-centered.

Within the types of training, some flexibility exists as to the methods. There are various forms of instructional methods:

- ▼ lecture—trainer-centered (telling someone about something)
- ▼ demonstration—trainer-centered (displaying how to do something)
- ▼ case study—learner-centered (giving a written history with a plot and characters to simulate a decision-making situation on the job)
- ▼ simulation—learner-centered (presenting an on-the-job event to provide learners an opportunity to develop their skills or discover concepts to improve their performance)
- ▼ panel discussion—learner-centered (selecting a group of experts to discuss and share their views on a given topic)
- ▼ virtual reality training—learner-centered (putting trainees in an artificial, three-dimensional environment to simulate an event to practice skills or knowledge)
- ▼ computer-based training—learner-centered (training through the use of a computer)
- ▼ on-the-job training—learner-centered (following a sequence of learning events presented by a supervisor or expert in a one-on-one situation).

▼▼▼

Aim for a variety in both method and media. It breaks up the learners' day and allows the message to appeal to the various learning styles.

▲▲▲

Training Roles

The most recognized role of the trainer is as a deliverer; therefore, one of the key competencies to acquire is presentation and facilitation skills. A trainer should be good at organizing and providing information so the attention of the audience is held and the information is accurately conveyed.

Training, however, is much more, and in many situations the presenting role is one of the least important. Merely considering the five stages in the training cycle (prepare the learner, present the information, practice the activity, provide feedback, and provide opportunities for integrating) indicates that numerous roles are demanded. For example, the skills for analyzing needs are different from the skills for presenting, and the skills for designing a course are different from the skills for evaluating, and the skills for writing resource material are different from the skills for managing groups. Many more roles have to be performed, both in and out of the group situation.

Not all trainers can be excellent at all of their roles. They should play to their strengths, while finding ways to combat their weaknesses. They should either concentrate on developing the weaknesses or ensure that other people who have strengths in these areas are involved in the training—other team members, class participants, external technicians, or subject matter experts. Whichever method they use, trainers need to make sure the training goes well and the learners learn and leave as satisfied customers.

▼▼▼

Some of the roles required by the trainer are presenter, subject matter expert, mentor, coach, counselor, facilitator, teacher, innovator, role model, technician, diffuser, persuader, seller, and catalyst.

▲▲▲

Training Presentation Skills Assessment

What is your intention? What do you hope to achieve? What content or message do you want to get across? Answering these questions calls for a review of three evaluation questions that need to be asked in order to design and deliver a purposeful training presentation (see table 2-2.). Complete the skills assessment in table 2-2 to evaluate your training presentation.

Individuals attend trainings to acquire knowledge and, in some cases, to share information with individuals in their organizations. Given this generalization of a typical audience profile, the main role of the trainer is that of a facilitator. While most of this role will be undertaken when the group is actually together, much of it also takes place elsewhere, for example, at the needs analysis stage, where trainers facilitate the identification of training needs and the release of individuals for training.

Within the training situation, most of the roles of the facilitator fall into three categories: the subject matter expert, the methods expert, and the group manager.

Subject Matter Expert

Learners expect trainers to know something about the subject, and the more the trainers know and communicate that knowledge, the more their credibility increases. Thus, it is an important part of their development to update their knowledge of the field.

Table 2-2. Training presentation skills assessment.

Level	Evaluation	Yes	No
There are four purposes for training: 　a. to train on skills, knowledge, or abilities 　b. to retrain 　c. to present and test 　d. to inform.	1. Do I define the basic training purpose?		
Here are some questions to ask to help identify the end result: 　a. Is it achievable? 　b. Is it a present or ultimate objective? 　c. Is it measurable? 　d. Is there evidence that the material is transferred back on the job?	2. Do I define the training objectives?		
The main point of the training intervention is successful training so that the content is implemented on the job.	3. Do I present the content to match the objectives?		

Learners, however, do not expect trainers to know everything. Nobody can be a complete fountain of knowledge; and if trainers don't know something, they should admit it. They should recognize any expertise within the group and use it when appropriate. Also, with a specialized field, they should consider bringing in a subject matter expert for a group chat, which not only gives expert input of knowledge but also exposes learners to a change of style, which is often beneficial.

▼▼▼

Trainers should not create such an aura of expertise that they become unapproachable. Credible experts with the human touch are far more respected. For most people, merely being natural is the best way to achieve this.

▲▲▲

Methods Expert

Part of a trainer's role is to exercise sound, professional judgment as to the best method the learners need and to accommodate all the learning preferences.

There are numerous instructional methods available, and trainers should be familiar with most and feel comfortable and competent with a few. They should watch other trainers and learn from them, take occasional risks, and be open to experimenting.

Group Manager

This is an area in which facilitation skills are most obvious. Trainers require a high level of interpersonal skills to be able to manage (not control) a group. The style and role can change from motivator to leader to counselor, according to the situation.

Trainers must be sensitive to group atmosphere and mood as well as to the individuals attending. They need to have some understanding of individual and group psychology, although they do not need to be experts.

Training Evaluation

Everyone has an interpretation of what training success means. Because there are many variables to consider that affect the training process, there are many ways to measure trainings to see if they are both effective and useful. Learners may see a particular course as successful because it was fun, included a lot of nice people, and had tasty snacks. Or learners may rate the course highly, but when it is time to apply the skills, the transfer of training did not take place.

One way to measure successful training transfer is through Kirkpatrick's (1979) four levels of evaluation: reaction, learning, behavior, and results (table 2-3). If trainers use the evaluation concept to assist them in designing the training topic and writing assessment tests when developing the course materials, they will ensure that training transfer does take place during the learning process.

Notice that each level of this evaluation model measures a different aspect of training and how the training can affect a different level of the organization. Trainers can

▼▼▼

The question to constantly ask is, "Was training successful?" This question will be answered differently based upon the evaluation level.

▲▲▲

Table 2-3. Kirkpatrick's Four Levels of Evaluation.

Level	Evaluation	Description
1	Reaction	How did the learner react to the training course?
2	Learning	How well did the learner apply the new skills or knowledge?
3	Behavior	What changes in job behavior resulted from the training?
4	Results	What were the results of training on the organization?

Source: Donald L. Kirkpatrick and James D. Kirkpatrick, *Evaluating Training Programs: The Four Levels,* 3d. ed. (San Francisco: Berrett-Koehler, 2006).

manage or design evaluation techniques to measure success only at Level 1 and Level 2. To measure success at Level 3, trainers must rely on feedback from the supervisor or employee. Measurement of success at Level 4 requires completion of a comprehensive needs analysis. Once training has been completed, trainers can determine if those needs have been addressed successfully. See chapter 11 for a more complete discussion of Kirkpatrick's evaluation levels.

Summary

Training is becoming more widely accepted and recognized as a way to enable individuals to cope with change. Through training, individuals can learn how to accept responsibility for their own shortcomings and developmental needs in order to manage their careers wisely. Attendance at training provides learners with an opportunity to see themselves as part of a larger organization and more effectively identify their significance and need for effective contribution.

Check-Up Exercise

1. Think about trainers you have observed or worked with.
    a. What were their strengths?
    b. What were their developmental needs?
    c. What made them successful?
    d. What were their unsuccessful situations?
    e. What did they not do well?
    f. What did you learn from them?

g. What method of learning did you most enjoy? Why?

h. What does the method you most like tell you about developing your own learning style?

i. If there was a training team, how did the trainers complement each other?

2. Think about three training situations you have been involved in.

a. What were the roles played by the trainers?

b. How did the trainers help learning?

c. What could have been done better to improve learning?

Instructional and Learning Strategies

Organizations now recognize that training is an important element for investing in their workforce. Every year the selection of appropriate training methods, learning materials, and instructional formats becomes more challenging because organizations demand to see a return on their investment.

This chapter provides opportunities for trainers to understand why and how to design and develop instructional strategies. In addition, the chapter explains how to use the most widely accepted instructional formats including tips and techniques for designing and delivering accelerated and distance learning.

Training Variables and Instruction

Designing training requires planning and organization skills. The best way to achieve an organized and structured training is to design training while considering the training variables.

The term *training variables* covers various essential components that need to be included in a training design and delivery. The word *variable* means an element that plays a specific role at a specific time. There are three distinct variables trainers need to include in design strategy: training purpose levels; learner levels and trainer roles; and trainer roles.

Variable 1: Training Purpose Levels

The purpose of this variable is to force trainers to think about the type of training they are designing and delivering. There are four training purpose levels: awareness, knowledge, motivation, and skill or behavior change. By incorporating the four levels, as shown in figure 3-1, in the design, trainers can be confident that they have solid, successful training events.

Awareness training enlightens learners and improves their awareness levels and attitudes on a specific subject. This level of training does not seek to change the learners' behaviors. An example of this is a new organization benefits training.

Knowledge training is designed to give learners improved knowledge about a specific issue. The amount of knowledge gained in the training can be specific and tested. An example of this is a new product training.

Motivation training is designed to move learners to take specific actions that have specific benefits to someone or something. An example of this is an organizational change training.

Skill or behavior change training is designed to give learners the tools to perform differently on the job. Specific skill changes are taught, and the results of the training can be tested. The skills can include either personal (for example, time management or keyboard skills) or group (for example, team problem-solving processes) activities. An example of this is a social skills training.

Each training presentation should be created to fulfill one of the purpose levels. Once the training topic and instructional strategy are defined, trainers build on the road map using the other variables. The training purpose levels variable provides the focus for the training.

Figure 3-1. Training purpose levels.

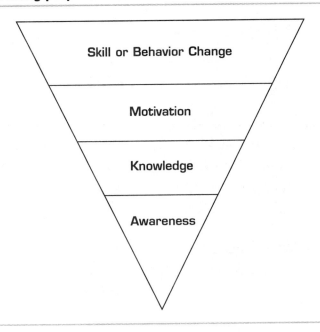

Variable 2: Learner Levels and Trainer Roles

To explain this variable and how to use the concept to design and deliver training, trainers should remember that there are two dynamics that are involved in teaching adults. The first dynamic is the relationship that trainers have with the training concepts they are delivering, the learner, and the instructional process trainers are using (that is, the trainer role). The second dynamic is the content that is delivered (that is, the amount of data learners need to know, or learner level). The most important factor for this dynamic is trainers' judgment as they determine how much information and direction they provide the learners to the learning situation and the learning cycle.

When trainers design their training material and develop their instructional strategies, they should keep in mind that some learners need a lot of information (written, spoken, and multimedia), whereas others have mastered the content and need only to occasionally check in with the facilitator. The degree to which trainers emphasize lecture and content and the amount of learning activity is an instructional design decision.

Variable 3: Trainer Roles

There is no one way to design and deliver training; however, there is an instructional design strategy that trainers can use to define their role. The four roles that trainers can play are instructor, coach, facilitator, or consultant. Each trainer role requires the trainer to make a decision as to what is required during the learning event, as shown in table 3-1. The appropriate choice of role is based on the trainer's assessment of the learners and the amount of content and direction required to achieve the training outcome as defined by the lesson's learning objective statement. For example, if a trainer is introducing new material, and learners need a substantial amount of direction to understand and master the material, the trainer role assumed would

Table 3-1. Trainer roles.

Facilitator	Coach
• provides guidance although not involved in the process • helps learners gain knowledge from experience and each other	• provides guidelines, help, and direction • watches from the sidelines • observes, practices, and gives corrective feedback
Consultant	**Instructor**
• acts as an adviser	• provides detailed direction, foundational material, and structured learning events for learners to master the topic

be one of instructor. As the learners become more familiar with the learning content, and require less direction, the trainer assumes a different role.

Learning Style Preferences

Although there is no one comprehensive learning style theory that all researchers and trainers agree upon, they do agree that individuals learn differently and learners exhibit preferences for processing the information to be learned.

The preferences most often identified have been classified as processing preferences, perceptual preferences, and other learning preferences that relate to the environment and emotions. This information is helpful when trainers make decisions about instructional strategies, the levels of the learners, and the role of the trainer.

Processing Preferences

There are two ways that people process information. People who are *global* processors want to comprehend the big picture first and then work on comprehending the details that support the big picture, while people who are *analytic* (or linear) processors want to comprehend the details first and work systematically toward grasping the big picture. The terms *global* and *analytic* have also been described respectively as right brain and left brain, sequential and simultaneous, and deductive and inductive.

Perceptual Preferences

There are three preferences that people use to involve themselves with information presented: visual, auditory, and kinesthetic. According to Rita Dunn, director of St. John's University Center for the Study of Learning and Teaching Styles, the learning style distribution in an average group is 30–40 percent visual, 20–30 percent auditory, and 30–50 percent kinesthetic (Filipczak, 1995).

Other Learning Preferences

Other preferences identified are the learning environment—for example, noisy versus quiet—and emotionality of the learner, such as motivational elements and psychological factors.

Developing Instruction Around Learning Styles

Gathering information about an audience can be an important step in developing effective instructional strategies. To determine how the audience will learn best, trainers should assess the various learning styles of the training participants to help them design appropriate instructional strategies.

▼ ▼ ▼

With some background and understanding of learning style models, trainers can determine an individual's learning style through various techniques:

- Interview the person, and inquire about learning preferences.
- Observe the learner in learning environments.
- Evaluate what have been positive and effective learning experiences versus what have been negative and ineffective ones.
- Review the completed self-assessment questionnaire.

▲ ▲ ▲

Most researchers believe that trainers should understand more than one learning style model so they can employ the learning style model that is most appropriate for each learning situation. Whatever learning style assessment approach is used, trainers should consider how to incorporate the information they gather about their audiences. Researchers have focused on three areas in which to apply learning style information: self-awareness, course design, and instructional strategies.

Self-Awareness

Several researchers recommend that trainers and learners go through assessment exercises so they all have a greater self-awareness of their own learning styles. Trainers need to know what preferences they exhibit, because their preferences may affect how they present information to learners. Learners need increased self-awareness in these areas to help them be better learners.

Course Design Instructional Strategies

In deciding how to use the audience's learning style preferences, there are three possible strategies. The first strategy is to design a course focused on individual learning style strengths and preferences. The second strategy is to design a course to help individuals improve on the weaker aspects of their learning styles, thus enabling them to become more flexible and adaptable to the variety of teaching methods they encounter. The third strategy is to use a combination and variety of teaching methods.

Matching Methods and Learning Outcomes

Because instructional methods differ in their ability to influence knowledge, skills, and attitudes, trainers must be able to evaluate a method's utility and ability and make informed decisions about its use in their training.

Training is all about providing instruction for the learners to acquire new skills or knowledge to enhance job performance. When trainers think about acquiring new knowledge, they should remember that knowledge is acquired at three levels:

1. **declarative**—a process for acquiring knowledge when the learner stores the information for future use
2. **procedural**—a process for acquiring knowledge when the learner understands how the information presented can be applied
3. **strategic**—a process used when there is a need for planning, monitoring, or revising a goal-directive activity.

There will be times when trainers have to design a training to include learning objectives in more than one area. To accomplish this task, trainers should combine several instructional methods into an integrated whole, because no single method can do everything well. These various instructional methods can be divided into two broad learning categories: cognitive and behavioral. Either the behavioral or the cognitive instructional method can be used to change attitudes, although each does so through different means. Cognitive methods are best for imparting knowledge or development, and behavioral methods are best for honing skills.

Cognitive Methods

Cognitive instructional methods provide verbal or written information, demonstrate relationships among concepts, or provide the steps for how to do something. These methods stimulate learning through their effect on cognitive processes and are associated most closely with changes in knowledge and attitude.

Behavioral Methods

Behavioral instructional methods provide learners practice using the newly acquired behavior in a real or simulated event. The methods stimulate learning through behavior and are best used for skill acquisition or behavior change.

In assessing what methods to use, trainers should evaluate in the following five areas:

1. Are the models reliable and valid?
2. Is there widespread practitioner use?
3. Is there extensive research behind the models?
4. Can I visit places that are using the models I am interested in?
5. Can I obtain training so I know how to use individual styles to obtain increased achievement?

Accelerated Learning Techniques

Several years ago, an association created a new training for trainers. Much of the project time was spent researching the principles of learning, exploring how the mind worked, and defining the concept of multiple intelligences and how the concept applied to training design.

The final course design was creative, with color icons on pages instead of words, multicolored wall charts created to hang in the training room that told the story of the training program, and music played during the training session, specifically, in the beginning, ending, break, and project times. This course continues to ensure that every learner walks away from this class learning something and having fun doing so.

Structured learning events may include accelerated learning techniques such as the following:

- back-home application
- brainwriting and brainstorming
- case study
- collaborative activity
- concert review
- environing material
- in-class demonstration
- prework
- reading assignment
- structured note taking
- skills and knowledge test
- self-assessment

Such varied techniques provide opportunities to plan, organize, and prepare trainings efficiently and economically. Structured events provide the road map for trainers to use to develop their content as well as provide techniques and tips for them to be successful when delivering the training event.

Back-Home Application

Definition. Participants are given an in-class opportunity to practice what they have learned by applying the learned concepts to an existing back-home problem.

Directions. Each participant writes a short synopsis of a back-home problem. Next, each participant presents the issue to the group. By group consensus, one problem is selected to be used as a model problem to apply the new techniques that were presented during the class. The group works as consultants to the participant who has the issue, thus helping that person apply the concepts and skills from the group to use back home.

Tools and Tips. Here are suggestions to consider when managing this learning process:

1. Use the steps in sequence.
2. Use examples to reinforce learning with direct application to the learners' situations.
3. Ask the class to share back-home plans.
4. Make frequent referrals to back home during other activities.

Brainwriting and Brainstorming

Definition. Participants record ideas, advancing previous ideas (brainwriting) or listing ideas (brainstorming).

Directions. For brainwriting, write two questions on two flipcharts. Have participants silently write their answers to each question on an individual basis. Give a time limit. After the participants have recorded their answers, process the responses or have two participants process the questions. An example of a question is "Training is successful when..." and the opposing question would be "Training is unsuccessful when...."

Use mindmapping as a device for problem solving or decision making. The technique is based on the idea that many people find it helpful to dump out a lot of ideas in a very short period of time and then organize the ideas. Have participants draw a circle in the middle of a paper. Put the key concept in the center, and branch out from the middle of the circle.

The brainstorming process allows participants to generate a list of responses to the question or activity, in a given timeframe. This process provides the participants the opportunity to provide quick responses without being hindered by prejudgment. The point of brainstorming is to generate a lot of responses. Once the list of responses is produced, the participants review the list and delete responses that are not considered feasible.

Tools and Tips. Here are suggestions to consider when managing differences of opinion:

1. Ensure that groups follow rules; monitor the groups closely; remember silence!
2. Don't allow verbal criticism (brainstorming).
3. Keep groups and papers moving. Keep them on track (brainwriting).
4. Point out that both brainwriting and brainstorming allow one person's idea to trigger another person's related idea.

5. Point out that brainwriting allows participants to build on ideas without the threat of criticism.
6. Use colored markers, and post charts.
7. Try using mindmapping in brainwriting.

Case Study

Definition. Participants work to solve a problem similar to ones they face back home. A case study usually has multiple parts (plot, characters, issue, and setting) and various solutions and is processed as the parts are completed.

Directions. Write a narrative, one or two paragraphs. Include detail about the situation, the characters involved, and the rationale for why this is an issue. Do not write suggested solutions; the point of the case study is to invite others to discuss the various options.

Tools and Tips. Here are suggestions to consider when completing case studies:

1. Monitor groups, and answer questions.
2. Don't let the groups go too long without intervening.
3. Don't use cases that are not related to the businesses of the participants.
4. Point out that case studies encourage creative problem solving.
5. Help participants learn from one another.
6. Post flipcharts from groups around the room so all groups can learn from one another.

Collaborative Activity

Definition. Participants work together to teach one another concepts, solve problems, or advance the learning objectives for the training event.

Directions. Create application exercises in the participant manual. The focus of the exercises is to invite learners to review the important points in the lesson. These exercises can include quizzes, scenarios, matching terms, or essays. The important point for this activity is that the group members can work independently, and then work together to pool their answers. This activity provides an opportunity for participants to ask for clarification and learn from others in the group; thus, each participant is becoming self-reliant while functioning as a team player.

Tools and Tips. This activity is a good way to review material and introduce the concept of the learning group, which means everyone helps one another.

1. Collaboration should pervade the entire training event.
2. Learning is more effective in small groups with supportive and helpful members.

3. Individual learning focuses on only the individual and does not provide for effective feedback. Individuals tend to emphasize their own mistakes, faults, and weaknesses, sometimes blowing them out of proportion because they have no comparisons.

4. Remember, there's strength in numbers.

Concert Review

Definition. Trainers can review materials, periodically using music, presentations, wall charts, flipcharts, movements, or verbal reviews.

Directions. This is a review activity. Tell participants that they are going to review the material covered thus far in the training and the number of concepts that have been presented. Have them number their papers accordingly.

Explain that the trainer is going to play music and at set intervals the trainer will put up an image that represents a concept that was presented during the training. Tell the participants that when they see the image, they are to write everything they know about the image until it disappears.

After the presentation is complete, the learners should collaborate with their groups to clarify and check the entries. This is a great way to have the group work together, as well as to promote the collaborative learning process.

Tools and Tips. The concert review approach to reviewing materials refers to the use of background music during review. The technique works for the three learning styles (visual, auditory, and kinesthetic) and the two ways people process information (linear and global). Some examples include

- ▼ **Visual**. The facilitator silently flips through overheads, flipcharts, or wall charts. Background music is an enhancer.
- ▼ **Auditory**. The facilitator reads specific review materials while background music plays.
- ▼ **Kinesthetic**. The group follows the facilitator around the room from item to item (wall charts, demonstration models, learning aids, displays) while music plays.
- ▼ **Linear**. The facilitator uses outlines of what's first, second, third, and so on.
- ▼ **Global**. The facilitator gives an overview.

Environing Material

Definition. The term *environing* refers to the learning environment. Trainers can ease the anxiety of adult learners by using themes for training and decorating the classroom according to the theme. Prewritten wall charts are an example of environing materials, also known as peripheral materials.

Directions. Decorating the learning room with interesting posters or wall charts that depict the major concepts being presented in the training can be a bonus for the learners and the facilitator. The topic for each of the wall charts could contain icons or words, display a manufacturing process, or summarize an important topic. Trainers should dress their training rooms to invite learners to be creative, holistic, or interactive with one another and the training material. Using attention-grabbers is the key to making these concepts blend with the training process and content delivery.

Tools and Tips. Environing materials are materials that make the learning environment more conducive to learning the concepts of the course. They include

1. wall charts and flipcharts
2. table decorations to fulfill a theme
3. mobiles and puzzles
4. candles and scents
5. anything that adds color, stimulation, and fun
6. funny bags to hold all of supplies for each team table
7. basket for the trainer table with more supplies, candy, and surprises.

Demonstration in Class

Definition. Participants observe or take part in a demonstration of the course concepts, techniques, skills, or tools.

Directions. Adults learn best by doing. Therefore, an opportunity to demonstrate something involves the participants learning the concept and preparing to teach the concept. One suggestion for managing this concept is to take a section of the course material, form learning groups, and have each group prepare a 10-minute presentation. To accomplish this task economically, the instructor should preassign the material to be reviewed and prepare an instruction sheet for each group to follow.

Tools and Tips. The demonstration process serves as a teach-back tool and can serve as a mechanism to encourage collaborative group work.

1. Use actual equipment and resources as much as possible.
2. Make demonstrations easy for everyone to see, hear, observe, practice, and so on.
3. Show trainees that you are an expert. This means that trainers may not be perfect at the skill, but, at the very least, they completely understand it.
4. Don't cut the process short. Teach all the steps.
5. Point out that demonstration allows hands-on learning.
6. Show participants how this technique reinforces auditory and visual learning. If time and situation permit, let participants demonstrate.

Prework

Definition. Participants do assignments prior to coming to class—it's part of the prepare step in the accelerated learning process (prepare, present, practice, and feedback).

Directions. Learners really like to receive an agenda so that they can get a sense of what they are going to do, how to do it, and what the expected results are. The prework provides the opportunity for learners to prepare for the session. It serves as a map of the adventure they will experience when they arrive at the training event.

Tools and Tips. Adult learners like to know where they are, where they are going, and how they will get there. The prework can serve as a mechanism to provide that direction.

1. Fun packages can include toys used in class, tee shirts, course logo stuff (pens, pencils, notebooks), video of skits, cartoons, and so forth.
2. Serious work packages can include questionnaires, preassessment instruments, prereading material, audiotapes, or videotapes.
3. Incentive-to-get-there packages can include course goals, course outline, testimonials from previous attendees, and statements of outcomes, among others.
4. If the course has a theme, theme the prework!
5. Mix media and color, action, and fun.

Reading Assignment

Definition. Participants are given evening or out-of-class assignments to supplement classroom materials and experiences.

Directions. Reviewing and reflecting on the information gathered in class is something that you should encourage all participants to practice. Give them time to make connections between the new content and information that they already know. Look over the goals and objectives of the course, and develop summary handouts or search for expert sources of materials—articles or case studies—to expand the learners' knowledge of the topics discussed.

Tools and Tips. The art of reading should be a skill that we continually practice. The reading assignments and report backs are vehicles to ensure that all the participants have read required materials. Remember that participants have lives outside of the training. Try to keep the assignments quick (short reviews previewing the next day's materials).

1. Make it memorable. Some people can learn a great deal by reading and homework; others hate it.
2. Ask participants to record their learning creatively.

3. Try memory maps or mindmaps.
4. Create a mobile or three-dimensional object.
5. Ask participants to make videotapes.

Structured Note Taking

Definition. Text materials are roughly outlined so participants know what's important and where to take notes. White space is provided for participants to add their own notes.

Directions. Review the materials that you are to present in a lecture, and decide which sections are highlights of the training. Develop a note sheet for the participants to use to record the important points during your content delivery process. This teaching process can be a video, demonstration, discussion, or presentation.

Tools and Tips. The structured note process is something that people do all the time in the form of recording thoughts or points in a meeting or developing a cheat sheet to remember points for a speech or presentation. The structured note process will assist the participants in remembering the important points of the presentation.

1. Design the courses to make everyone take notes once in a while.
2. Remember: It's kinesthetic.
3. Go slowly enough so everyone can get something on paper.
4. Don't put too much on the slides or overheads.
5. Don't use jargon that learners don't understand or can't spell.
6. Remember that note taking reinforces learning.
7. Have participants record in the participant guide, not on separate sheets of paper.

Skills and Knowledge Test

Definition. Tests are used to determine how much participants have learned while they were attending the training.

Directions. The importance of testing is to have participants reflect and recall information and to make the connections to their existing knowledge portfolio. The tests that trainers use should not be threatening but serve as a review. Prepare the tests, and put them in the participant manual in sections after the initial lesson or module. Trainers should use any test form they think appropriate—for example, fill in the blank, written response to a scenario or case study, or match the terms. Try to introduce the concept that tests can be fun and useful.

Tools and Tips. The tests are assessments, an opportunity to determine how well participants are grasping the information; therefore, make the tests collaborative and fun. Give prizes.

1. Daily review assessments work very well.
2. Make sure all material is relevant, and use tests for different learning styles, for example, kinesthetic, visual, or auditory.
3. Allow learners to re-take tests that are important to success.
4. Use testing creatively as a recall, for example, group quizzes with prizes.
5. Don't publicize everyone's score or make passing scores too high.
6. If you have never written a test, get help!
7. Participant-generated review questions add fun and show how much they are learning.

Self-Assessment

Definition. Participants use profiles, tests, or inventories of their current skill levels to check their progress and learning during the class.

Directions. Do not test for test's sake. Participants love opportunities to find out more about what they are doing well and not so well. If trainers are going to use the assessment technique, they should make sure that it is valid and meaningful. Trainers can buy assessment instruments or develop their own, using the content that they are delivering in the session. For example, if trainers are teaching the learners the instructional systems design model, they can write a scenario about a training department that receives a request for training and ask the learners to develop a response to the client that provides the steps they will take. This scenario provides real-world experience and also serves to review the material.

Tools and Tips. Either purchase or develop assessment instruments that correspond to or highlight the concepts you are teaching.

1. Provide opportunities for learners to learn more about themselves.
2. Suggest learners use similar assessments in their own classrooms.
3. Give learners fast and frequent successes.
4. Try pre- and posttests. This technique allows the learners to demonstrate to themselves what they have learned.
5. Back-home quizzes let the learners know that there are some positive things going on they may not be aware of.

Problem-Based Learning

Problem-based learning is an instructional method that challenges participants to learn by working together in groups to seek solutions to real-world problems. Use problem-based learning to prepare learners to think critically and analytically and to find and use appropriate learning sources. When trainers use the problem-based learning strategy as a teaching tool, they can transform a traditional lecture into a group-centered, problem-solving experience. The purpose of problem-based learning is to provide the learners with a hands-on learning approach (as shown in sidebar below)—a practical tool to use when writing real-life problems as content for training sessions.

To prepare for the problem-based learning session, pay close attention to detail, organization, and design and provide some built-in structure to manage the problem introduction, group dynamics, and summary product.

▼ ▼ ▼

Problem-based learning design template.

Introduction and Overview

Each person will have an opportunity to describe a problem for the group to solve. The exercise provides an opportunity for learners to work together to solve a real workplace problem.

1. Give the learners guidelines.
2. Instruct each group to elect a group leader. The group leader then has the responsibility to collect the problem statements from each member and read each proposed problem scenario to the group; the group adopts one problem statement to use throughout the training problem.
3. Allow ample time each day of the training sessions for groups to work on their chosen cases and report progress to the entire group.
4. Provide each group member with a sheet of printed questions to help the group arrive at a problem solution. Typically questions can be

   - What is the problem?
   - Who is involved?
   - What would you like to see happen?
   - What is the worst-case scenario if what you want for a solution doesn't happen?
   - What would the situation look like if the problem was resolved the way you consider appropriate?

In-Session Check-In

Assess the progress of the group problem-solving task at regular intervals. If necessary, interrupt group work to correct misconceptions or to make sure that the groups are all in sync with respect to the task and time allotted for the task.

Discussion Time

Allow time for total group discussion of the problem at the end of the problem-based learning session or at the beginning of the next session of your training event.

▲ ▲ ▲

Distance Learning

The anytime classroom and the virtual classroom are easy to confuse with one another. However, there are distinct differences. With distance learning, there are two main dimensions that are addressed: location and time. Both the anytime classroom and the virtual classroom address location; therefore, the course can be taken at several locations at the same time.

The anytime classroom also addresses time. As the name suggests, the instruction can be taken at any time. It is the most common approach to web-based instruction. Most of the communication involved in this form of distance learning is conducted over the World Wide Web or an organization's intranet. CD-ROM-based instruction can also be delivered so that it is available anytime.

The virtual classroom mode of distance learning can also be delivered over the web, although most versions now run on special voice or data networks. These networks are generally considered the web. The major distinguishing characteristic of the virtual classroom is that there is generally an online instructor in real time. As a result, instruction delivered via a virtual classroom is not available at any time.

There are five primary technologies used for distance learning, which are discussed below.

Remote Classroom (Interactive Television)

Instruction is delivered to clusters of learners who meet in a classroom environment physically separated from a centralized school or institution. Instruction may be delivered simultaneously to one or more classrooms. Information is presented to the group from the central school—usually through some form of video interface that includes the ability to display graphics. Comments and questions of learners in the remote classroom are transmitted back to the instructor in the central school by telephone or an audiovisual system.

Virtual Classroom (Synchronous Online Instruction)

Instruction is delivered to learners through their computers. All of the learners are connected to the network at the same time. The instructor has complete control over what the learners see and hear on their computers. The instructor can ask a question or make a comment. The instructor can even pass control to an individual learner who can comment orally, add to the common whiteboard display, or present a visual that the other learners can view. This approach emulates a classroom environment and is run electronically in real time, as if everyone were in the same room.

Anytime Classroom (Asynchronous CD-ROM Instruction)

Instruction is delivered to learners through their computers. The information is conveyed to their computers via a CD-ROM. Learners tend to work through the materials independently, setting their own schedules and pace of instruction.

Anytime Classroom (Asynchronous Online Instruction)

Instruction is delivered to learners through their computers. The information is conveyed to their computers via telecommunication lines and is considered web-based. Learners tend to work through the materials independently, setting their own schedules and pace of instruction.

Web-Based Training Programs

Because web-based training is a technology delivery system that provides training information, selecting the type of program requires trainers to make informed decisions. Weighing the needs assessment results, audience profile, outcome objectives, and level of evaluation should make deciding easier. Figure 3-2 offers a storyboard template for web-based trainings. There are three basic types of web-based training programs:

Type 1: Text and Graphic Web-Based Training

Type 1 training is sometimes referred to as the paper-based course (linear) that trainers mediate, meaning that they place the existing course on the web for selected learners to access. The design of the Type 1 format is a "page turner."

The design consists of boxes of text that are used similarly to those in a long email message. This text and graphics model is the place where many instructional designers start when developing web-based training because the format is simple to create and uncomplicated for the user.

Type 2: Interactive Web-Based Training

Type 2 training is an interactive training format. The purpose of this instructional design is to engage the learner with the training material. At a minimum, this design consists of application exercises, drag-and-drop, column matching, testing, and text entry.

This format presents more than just linear text and graphic presentations. It provides the learner with the option to interact with the program, content, and practice skills.

Figure 3-2. Storyboard template for web-based instruction.

Module Title: (List the course name and module or unit number)

Module Objective: (List the learning outcome)

Major Topics: (List the module or unit topics for the course)

1. Module 1 _____

2. Module 2 _____

3. Module 3 _____

Subtopics: (Optional section: if you use modules, you must include lessons in the modules, and therefore is no need for subtopics; however, if you use a "topic" as a label and do not designate a unit or module, then you should include subtopics.)

1. _____

2. _____

3. _____

Screen Content Design Template #1

Key Components and Subtopics: (Using the 10/70/20 Rule)

1. Ten percent of the presentation consists of an introduction (benefit of the training, objective statement, and transition to the next topic).

2. Seventy percent of the presentation consists of the content: topics or modules.

3. Twenty percent of the presentation consists of the conclusion and summary.

Opening and Instructions: (Introduction)
Key Topic and Subtopics: (Body)
Closing and Learner Test: (Summary)

Screen Content Design Template #2

Online Activities and Support Content (This is the section for your topic content.)

Balance (Include in each module.)

Type 3: Interactive Multimedia Web-Based Training

Type 3 training is interactive, using multimedia to deliver high levels of interactivity and providing a record-keeping option to manage the learning. The Type 3 format provides the learner the opportunity to mimic real life by providing immediate, real-life responses to the user.

Most programs that fall into this category allow the user to manipulate graphic objectives in real time, sometimes taking on the quality of game-playing or a drill exercise. An example of this is NASA's Space Shuttle Launch Simulation (www.ksc.nasa.gov/sim/launch/index2.html).

Summary

This chapter presented information on the instructional design process for organizing content and provided suggestions for delivery formats. Remember, a well-designed training means that trainers are halfway there to being outstanding in their presentations. The other half of the formula for success is their delivery strategy.

Trainers should teach what they know and know what they teach. They should be confident, organized, and well prepared when they tell learners what they know. Think of learning as a dialogue. Be an organized and informed communicator.

Check-Up Exercise

1. Identify the four training purpose levels, and give an example for each.
2. What are the four trainer roles?
3. List and describe three accelerated learning techniques.

Trainer Credibility

"Persuasion is achieved by the speaker's personal character when the speech is so spoken as to make us think him credible. We believe a good person more fully and more readily than others. There are three things which inspire confidence in character that induce us to believe a thing apart from the proof of . . . good sense, good moral character, and good will."

—Aristotle

The credibility characteristics put forth by Aristotle are important for any speaker and especially so for trainers. But before defining the qualities of a credible trainer, we must remember that not all the trainings that trainers do should be considered "training." The term *training* is used universally to define training sessions, but some training sessions are really an education session or an instructional session. People use the term *education* to describe all life experiences in which they learn. Yet, a series of particular experiences, perhaps using videotapes and city maps, that would be specifically focused on preparing someone to navigate city traffic would be considered *instruction*.

The term *training*, then, is used when those instructional experiences are focused on individuals acquiring very specific skills they will normally apply almost immediately. The term *trainer* assumes a variety of functions depending on the subject matter, the training technique, and the needs and learning styles of the learners.

Trainer as Leader

Psychologists have researched group behavior and discovered that when groups of individuals come together, the group selects someone to be given the authority to lead. Your role as trainer automatically identifies you as the leader. However, if you fail to fulfill that expectation as the leader of the group, you will be alienated from the group, leaving a vacuum to be filled by someone who possibly has come to the session reluctantly or who shows great resistance. Therefore, it is vital to establish your credibility as a competent practitioner immediately and continue to enhance that role throughout the training session.

There are a number of ways for you to assume the role of leader. This chapter is about how to accomplish that. To begin, consider the 10 rules of a leader that you can use to design your training, organize delivery, and manage sessions:

1. Set the agenda, and stay on track.
2. Teach to the objectives.
3. Protect the rights of each learner.
4. Listen for understanding.
5. Summarize important topics.
6. Review to promote making connections.
7. Focus the attention of the group.
8. Manage challenges to your authority.
9. Involve silent members.
10. Provide clear direction.

Set and Follow Agenda

The agenda is a trainer's contract with the learners. When learners come to a training, they want to know what they are going to learn, how they are going to learn it, and what the requirements are for completing the session. Your first responsibility as the leader is to set the agenda and follow the full instructions that are established. Next, present the learning objectives and lessons as defined in the agenda. Although learners will tolerate some deviation from the agenda, any change must be discussed and agreed upon at the beginning of the session.

Make sure there are regular, announced breaks. If you present a lecture or hold a discussion that lasts more than an hour, schedule a number of short breaks. If the training session consists of a balanced presentation of discussion, lecture, practice, and feedback, fewer breaks are necessary. Remember, part of your leadership role is to manage the time, the topics, and the instructional process.

Eliminate Distractions

A credible leader keeps the course from being sidetracked by distractions—both external and internal. External distractions are the reason most good training rooms are windowless. If the training room has windows, arrange the learning space so the learners face away from them.

Internal distractions can also be very frustrating. Poor seating, inadequate lighting, temperature, poor visibility, noise, interruptions, training rooms that are too large or too small, and strange smells are all situations that can contribute to learners being unhappy and distracted. Table 4-1 offers a checklist to examine the training environment.

Treat Learners with Respect and Fairness

Trainers should establish their roles as people who are honest, fair, and available. The group has given you the power to guide; do not abuse that power. Don't accept abusive language in the training environment or tolerate disrespect toward you or others in the group. Don't let one person dominate the group to the exclusion of the other participants. Finally, do not let learners be used as scapegoats, and do not allow either the majority or the minority to control the others.

Listen

Active listening is a skill that is difficult to master without practice. Remember that people cannot hear anything while they are speaking. Listen more, and learn more. People's minds constantly take in and store information. A mind is capable of processing information faster than others can speak, so both the trainer and the learners can easily be distracted from listening to one another. Fortunately, there is a way to improve the listening ability. By using three simple steps, you can improve your

Table 4-1. Checklist for examining the training environment.

Seating:	Are there adequate space, desks or tables, and comfortable chairs?
Lighting:	Is it too light or dim?
Temperature:	Is it too hot or cold?
Arrangement:	Can everyone see? Does everyone have a place to sit and a set of materials?
Breaks:	Are breaks scheduled one at least every 90 minutes?
Windows:	Are the windows shut with the blinds closed to minimize glare and distractions?

own listening skills and, by example, those of your learners as well. The three active listening steps include:

1. *Listen to summarize.* When participants are speaking, focus on their content and the context. What are they saying, and how are they saying it? What are their feelings, emotions, or intentions?

2. *Check for understanding.* When someone is speaking and you get lost in either the words or the intent, interrupt the conversation and ask for clarification or share your reflection on what you have heard and understood.

3. *Feed summary back.* When someone is responding, try to determine if the other person is hearing what you are intending to say.

Practicing the art of active listening provides an opportunity for you to really listen. In addition, when you focus your mind on a person or topic, you are less likely to be distracted. Also, you remember what was said much better because you are experiencing the conversation and not getting distracted. Finally, you win friends. Most people are happy that you interrupt the conversation, asking for clarification on their points. It suggests to the speakers that you are listening. Here are some helpful techniques to help you master active listening.

Strategizing

Active listening is not natural, and you may find it difficult to master the technique. You need to deliberately plan your strategy for engaging and listening effectively. During every training event, focus on your communication pattern and use the active listening technique.

Summarizing

At some point in your training session, stop and show how far you've come. Do this by summarizing what's been covered to that point, making connections with information that the participants have either already learned or already know. Summarizing the content gives them a feeling of progress. In effect, you are setting up sign posts in their learning journey so they can look back to see where they've been.

Reviewing

Frequent review sessions are critical to promote learning and understanding of what is being presented during your session. Reviewing is an opportunity to look back, to clarify, and to make connections with other information presented or with information the learner already knows. Frequent reviews of the topic presented will prepare learners to transition to the next topic in the training. Here are several review strategies:

1. Give pop quizzes.
2. Relate stories, or use metaphors.
3. Ask questions that invite discussion.
4. Walk through the topics covered.
5. Play review games.
6. Have each learning group write a question, and pass the questions to another group to write the answer response. (Make sure that those who wrote the questions have the answers, so they can judge the other groups' responses.)

Focusing

One of your critical tasks is to keep the group focused and on task. One way to consistently keep individuals on task is to use the agenda. The agenda should detail every major topic. Each topic you present should guide the learners to that section of the agenda. Another way of focusing is by referring to the learning objectives for each of your modules and lessons. A final strategy could be using visual aids, defining each topic and where you are in your presentation.

Trainers tend to lose focus during a training when they introduce group discussion. A success strategy for managing groups is to orchestrate the event. When a discussion begins, you are the moderator. Alternatively, appoint a learner to take on that task and you coach. If you invite a guest speaker, make sure that the speaker knows what to present, the purpose or objectives of that element of the agenda, the audience, the time allotted to the presentation and questions, their role during the event, and what role you will play during the visit. Establish an agenda, and stick to it. As the leader, inform the learners that the speaker will join them and provide details about what role they are to play, the importance of the topic, the speaker, and the learning outcome.

▼ ▼ ▼

Ask learners to respond to two questions: "What is clear?" and "What remains unclear?" This gets the learners to review the material in their own minds and make the needed connections between information that is stored and information that remains floating and has not made connection with existing topics.

▲ ▲ ▲

Responding

Getting individuals to participate in your training is a critical task. As a leader, the learners trust you and the role you play. They also trust you to manage the functions that were agreed upon in the agenda, course description, and objectives. The learners look to you to handle the teaching, classroom management, and administrative tasks with ease and efficiency.

Be ready for the unexpected. When someone challenges your leadership or disagrees with you, meet the challenge with a calm, open mind, using this formula:

▼ Greet the challenge openly.
▼ Smile warmly.
▼ Walk toward the challenger. (Never walk away or stand behind something that would signal that you want to hide.)
▼ Ask for clarification of the question, or state your understanding.
▼ If the issue is a genuine one, allow the person to explain.
▼ Conclude with some resolution (even if it means that you say you will have an answer when you check things out—just provide some deadline).
▼ When the challenger and others are relaxed and calm about the situation, move to the next session.

Ask and Answer Questions Skillfully

Every trainer should be skilled in the art of questioning, responding, and facilitating. Questions are used to facilitate learning, to clarify points, and to provide information.

Using Questions to Facilitate and Evaluate

Questions provide the opportunity for you to get the group moving and the learners involved with one another and the tasks. The use of questions can help you determine where the learners stand on an issue. You can use a question to draw out reticent learners or to cut off unnecessary discussions. Additionally, using questions can help you to hear multiple sides of an argument. There are seven types of questions that you can use in your training session:

1. **Open-Ended Questions**—asking for more elaboration
   "Can you tell me more about that?"
   "How did you feel when that happened?"
   "Thanks for that input. Can you say more?"
2. **Closed-Ended Questions**—asking for a short answer, with no elaboration
   "Have you ever experienced a group brainstorming session?"
   "Did you answer 'yes' to number one?"

3. **Echo Questions**—paraphrasing for clarity

   "In other words, you feel...?"

   "Can I paraphrase your comment by saying X?"

4. **Directed Questions**—attempting to get a specific answer

   "What did you like about the group activity?"

   "If you were to improve the skill practice, what would you do?"

5. **Loaded Questions**—seeking agreement through emphasis

   "We are moving forward; don't you agree?"

   "What did you like about the group activity?"

6. **Interrupting Questions**—interrupting the learner, activities, or discussions

   Parking Lot Approach: "Mark, can we post that question in the long-term parking lot?"

   Entire Group Approach: "Would it be helpful if we had only one conversation going at one time?"

7. **Rely Questions**—processing questions to get the group moving, put energy into discussions, or force individuals to take responsibility for their own learning

   There are four training scenarios that can easily integrate rely questions:

   ▼ *Facilitator-Participant* (single question directed at one participant)

   "Cheryl, you seem anxious to share what happened in your group. Can you tell us about it?"

   ▼ *Facilitator-Group* (one question, directed at the group helps to stimulate thought and interaction)

   "How did the rest of you react to that?"

   ▼ *Participant-Facilitator-Different Participant*

   Participant: "I was reluctant to start the exercise. Is that common?"

   Facilitator: "Let's find out. Mary, were you reluctant to begin?"

   ▼ *Participant-Group or Participant-Another Participant* (direct question that does not go through facilitator)

   Be careful of this schematic. This can get out of hand, and you may lose your leader control!

   Participant: "Bud, what do you think?"

   Facilitator: "Did that happen to anyone else?"

▼▼▼

The most important ingredient is trust. If you can create a climate for an open exchange, you will be asked questions almost as often as you ask them yourself.

▲▲▲

Responding to Questions

Here are five steps to follow in responding to questions:

1. Listen.
2. Acknowledge the question.
3. Ask for clarification.
4. Answer the question.
5. Verify that your answer is acceptable.

When following this process, be careful not to disparage the person who asked the question. Also, don't try to answer a question that you can't. Tell the learners that you don't know the answer, but that you will get them an answer. When you answer a question, don't get lost in your response; stay focused, and answer the question. However, if you are asked a question that tends to put you in a spot, remain neutral, and say, "That's interesting." This response conveys your interest, yet keeps you from immediately answering. Once you have listened and clarified the question, you can move to answering it and verify that you have addressed it sufficiently.

Questions can be powerful instruments to manage the learning, and questions can be used as clarifying tools. Use them wisely and often to excite learning and to evaluate how much is being understood and accomplished.

Proxemics

The word *proxemics* comes from the same word root as *proximity*. Proxemics is the study of the use of space. It covers everything from positioning offices in a building to choosing the best place to sit on a crowded beach. Elements of proxemics include room arrangements, which are covered in Chapter 10 and in the Tool Kit, and how you position yourself and your audience in your training environment (figure 4-1).

In Western culture, leadership assumes and is awarded more space. People create invisible boundaries that come into play in varying circumstances. People regard proximities of up to one-and-one-half feet as intimate. In normal circumstances, people allow only those they care about to be so close. On public transportation or in other crowded situations, people break down this invisible barrier but often feel intense discomfort at doing it.

In contrast, the space from one-and-one-half feet to four feet is regarded as casual, personal space. This is the normal space, and people will sit or stand to talk to each other at about this distance from one another.

Figure 4-1. Presenter zone.

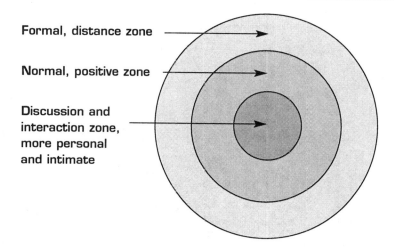

Formal, distance zone

Normal, positive zone

Discussion and
interaction zone,
more personal
and intimate

The distance that concerns most trainers is the area of 12 feet. This is formal, social distance. Most important, it is the distance in the formal training seminar that trainers maintain between the nearest learners and themselves. When they move closer, trainers create discomfort. It is interpreted as either an invitation for greater intimacy or an authoritative encroachment on a learner's personal space.

All cultures have unwritten rules of behavior, but the boundaries and responses to violations vary considerably. When training non-Americans, trainers discover the limits and rules of the learners' barriers. In reality, people stake out territories and barriers within and around them. This is why learners return to the same seat day after day and feel uncomfortable if someone else takes the seat.

As the trainer, use your space. If you wish to give an impression of strong leadership, walk around the training room, among the learners, check how they are doing, sit with work groups, and lend a hand. Most people are not consciously aware of space so you can use these rules to control your training environment without creating friction during the event.

Five-Star Trainer Credibility

As the training leader, convey a strong message that you are in charge, that you have been where the learners are, and that you know what you are talking about. The initial question that most learners ask about you is who you are. They need your identification, and they have a need to trust and identify with you. When you begin your session, think about these five questions that the learners have on their minds during the first 10 minutes of the session:

1. Can they identify with you?
2. Are you one of them?
3. Are you credible?
4. Are you knowledgeable?
5. Can they trust you to be right?

One bit of folk wisdom passed down among trainers holds that learners tend to evaluate trainers in the first 60 seconds of their sessions. If learners are not sure how they feel about trainers and their competence, they will hold off judgment for a while, but those first few moments at the beginning of the session are critical in their decision making. Therefore, start with a powerful opening.

Provide a short welcome. In the welcome statement, give an overview of the topics and suggest something that might motivate them to listen, some benefit to their learning journey. One of my favorite motivating techniques is, "I guarantee that if you participate, you will be able to apply 80 percent of what you learn immediately!"

You are always on trial in two areas: identification and credibility. You must get the identification issue settled at the beginning of your training session. Use what they already know and what they want to know as a starting point for your preparation stage. Acknowledge the value of what they will be learning and its importance to their growth and development.

After you have identified with the audience and established your credibility, ask learners for their input about the course objective and conduct a brief audience needs assessment. Write responses on a flipchart. Review the list, and respond to the themes. Explain how the course will be conducted if there are topics that you recorded on the list that are not going to be covered during the session; don't ignore the issue.

Next, build a mental bridge for the learners by focusing on the topics to determine what is known and unknown and illustrate how the information fits with their existing knowledge portfolio. Also, use your experience to illustrate points that add to your credibility.

Remember, in every training, three distinct phases of instruction and audience response emerge. Here is how a structured session is designed using the phases of credibility as the focus:

▼ Initial credibility occurs before the training event begins. It is based on the organization's reputation, the trainer's reputation, and anything that the participants have heard about the course or the trainer.

▼ Derived credibility occurs during the training because the learners are continually evaluating the trainer's credibility. It can increase or decrease during the training session.

▼ Terminal credibility exists in the learners' minds after the training session is completed. It is based on what they saw, heard, or experienced during the training.

Each phase has specific elements that trainers must cover in their presentations. Although these three phases appear to be simple and constitute a process that learners go through unconsciously, it's important to remember they are the natural flow of instruction.

Another important aspect of personal training style is the "This is me!" element. One of the best ways to establish your identity and credibility is to present yourself in the framework of the Five-Star Personal Credibility Model: character, personality, competence, intention, and dynamism. Each of the five stars represents a part of your persona that the learners will observe. It is important for you to examine each component of the five-star model, reflect, and act. These elements, described below, should be a natural part of your human spirit. You just have to remind yourself to bring them to training each time!

Character

Character denotes high moral behavior. It means acting as a positive role model in the areas of ethics and integrity. For instance, trainers set the example of not responding to organization gossip and negative discussions about the organization, executives, managers, or trainees.

Personality

Personality in the training room translates into good delivery skills. It is the ability to laugh at oneself, maintain a positive attitude, display empathy, and exhibit forward-thinking thoughts.

Competence

Competence is the ability to do the job. It includes a trainer's qualifications, knowledge, and experience in the subject matter. It also is displayed in the trainer's presentation and facilitation skills.

Intention

Intention refers to the trainer's motive. It is derived from the learners' attitudes as to why the trainer is there, the trainer's intentions toward them, and the training course.

Dynamism

Dynamism is closely related to personality. It is the trainer's self-confidence level and charisma.

Presentation Style

Clothing, quotes, and nonverbal and verbal communication are important elements that add to your trainer credibility. Establishing the right image is a critical first step in establishing rapport with your audience.

Clothing

Ask yourself: Do my clothes add or detract from the impression I want to make? Whether you like it or not, your attire speaks volumes about you. A tip: Simple is better; understated is even better. Dress and appearance are the critical aspects of communicating who you are, and because 90 percent of your body is covered with clothing, the way you dress is important.

Quotes, Tales, and Resources

Quotes add credibility to your presentation. You can use a business quote, company information quote, or subject matter quote. Tales are your own stories, and they say you have been there and done that! Exciting resources are fundamental to credibility; using or quoting resources tells your audience that you have researched the topic.

Nonverbals

Who hasn't heard time and again that actions speak louder than words? It's true. People are always sending messages through their bodies, even when they're not speaking. Your body will communicate the following to your audience:

▼ your sincerity
▼ your enjoyment in making the presentation
▼ your belief in what you are communicating
▼ your interest in your audience and that you care about them
▼ your confidence in the situation and control of it.

Your goal is to use gestures purposefully, not randomly. To the extent possible, do the following:

▼ Control your gestures without being stiff.
▼ Be spontaneous without being contrived.
▼ Be dramatic without being theatrical.

▼ ▼ ▼

Your dress should reflect STATHUZ, which means to check everything before you go on!

> S = Snapped
> T = Tied
> A = Appropriate
> T = Tucked in
> H = Hidden
> U = Unsoiled
> Z = Zipped

▲ ▲ ▲

Let your body speak naturally just as you would in a conversation. Erect and relaxed posture conveys poise and confidence. Graceful, fluid movements convey purpose and thought, and precise and spontaneous gestures convey life and meaning.

The things trainers do speak louder than what they say! Their nonverbal behavior says a lot about what they are thinking. Look at some of the obvious nonverbal cues trainers use.

Eye Contact

The eyes have it! Eye contact remains vital throughout the entire interaction. Contact with learners conveys trust, interest, and concern. The cabbage head (eyes and face have no expression) concept doesn't work in one-on-one communication or in small groups; trainers have to really look at individuals!

Most trainers tend to favor one side of the room. Determine your favorite, and then make an effort to look at the other side.

Throughout your presentation, maintain eye contact with the entire audience. Avoid focusing on only a few people or on one side of the room. At all times, your eye contact should be natural and smooth and should not follow a set pattern. Eye contact is your most powerful body language. The simple act of looking a person squarely in the eye is more persuasive than a hundred words.

Look at one person and hold eye contact with that person until you get a response. Then move to another person. Keep doing this with people all around the room. If you did not have an opportunity to mingle with the audience before being introduced, then pick friendly faces as the first ones with whom to make eye contact. After you have warmed up and you sense the trainees are with you, focus on less friendly faces.

Handshake

A firm handshake means you are confident and in control. The first thing to think about in a handshake is whether or not it creates the impression that you intended? Is your handshake strong and firm? Does it convey enthusiasm and that you care to make the connection?

▼▼▼

Shake hands with both men and women in the same way. Do not shake hands with women by holding only the ends of their fingers. A firm grip is required.

▲▲▲

Posture

Your posture speaks volumes. Stand tall and with confidence. It's like Mom used to say, "Stand up straight!" Standing straight is good for your body and your mind. Remember, stand with your feet flat on the floor, and relax the neck and shoulders; standing tall makes a difference in your outlook!

Facial Expression

Your audience will assume the emotions you project. If your face shows excitement, your audience will begin to feel excited. If you look dour or afraid, your audience will begin to reflect that.

As with body language, facial expressions must always be appropriate. And while smiling is almost always recommended to connect you to your audience, if you are talking about a tragedy or making a demand, smiling would be inappropriate.

Check your facial expressions for animation, friendliness, naturalness, and appropriateness.

Movements and Gestures

Move around, taking multiple steps (one or two makes you look unsure). If you are thinking about gestures, you're overdoing it. Try to keep your hands empty. If you need a microphone, use a cordless one so you don't trip. Tape electrical cords to the floor so you don't fall.

Verbals

A strong pleasant voice is one of your greatest assets as a speaker. Breathing has a lot to do with the strength of your voice. You give yourself the best chance for success by

▼▼▼

Remember that your face is easy to control: Change your mindset, and smile more often. Try to remember to keep a neutral facial expression when you are angry or upset. Your smile is the most important thing that you wear; be sincere and generous—your smile could be the only one that these individuals receive today.

▲▲▲

standing up straight with your stomach tucked in so the diaphragm gets the support it needs to enable your lungs to fill deeply with air. Posture supplies the diaphragm the support it needs. A good speaking voice is

- ▼ pleasant and conveys warmth
- ▼ natural and reflects your personality
- ▼ dynamic and gives an impression of strength without being loud
- ▼ expressive and reveals shades of meaning and emotion
- ▼ articulate and makes it easy to understand what you are saying.

Check for the following when delivering your presentation:

- ▼ **Volume.** Is your voice audible, appropriately strong, and variable for emphasis?
- ▼ **Pitch.** Is your voice low pitched and melodic, conveying color?
- ▼ **Pace.** Do you speak neither too fast nor too slowly, without hesitations or jerks? Do you speak smoothly, fluently, and with deliberately varied speed?
- ▼ **Articulation.** Do you mumble, speak lazily, or mispronounce words?
- ▼ **Vocal quality.** Is your voice nasal, breathy, harsh, raspy, or lifeless?
- ▼ **Vocal variety.** Is your voice dull, strained, or lacking in emotion? Is your voice varied in pitch, volume, timing, and inflection, conveying emotion and vitality?

Welcome your participants with a firm handshake. Introduce yourself by name, and indicate that you will be the trainer for the session. Ask their names, and try to call them by their names immediately as it will help you to begin the relationship-developing phase.

Summary

This chapter presents two themes. The first theme is to define and describe what credible trainers are and what leadership qualities they should possess and manage.

The second theme is presentation credibility. There are a variety of techniques and tools that trainers can use to design their training events for success. Yet, the real key to success is how to plan, organize, and conduct trainings that are appropriate, focused, and meaningful to the learner.

Check-Up Exercise

1. Identify the 10 rules of a leader.
2. Describe the credibility characteristics of a five-star trainer.
3. What are two types of questions you can use in trainings to manage the training process?
4. What does the term *proxemics* mean to you, as a trainer?

▼ **Part II**

Designing a Training Program

The Multistep Training System Model

This section of the book provides a process to design and develop training programs. The multistep training system model is an easy-to-use guide that will help in all types of trainings. The purpose of establishing a training system in an organization is to ensure you design programs that

▼ respond to the organization's business needs
▼ are educationally sound
▼ have measurable product learning.

The Training System Model

Use the training system model, as shown in figure 5-1, as a guideline for developing new training programs or revising existing training programs. The six-stage model—business justification, analysis, design, development, implementation, and evaluation—follows a systems approach to planning, preparing, conducting, and evaluating training programs. Each stage involves specific techniques from the field of instructional technology. For example, the information you obtain through a needs analysis becomes the starting point for obtaining job analysis data. Then you use the information you obtain from the job analysis to determine the instructional objectives.

▼▼▼

By following the multistep training system model, you will be on the road to providing successful trainings.

▲▲▲

Figure 5-1. Training system model.

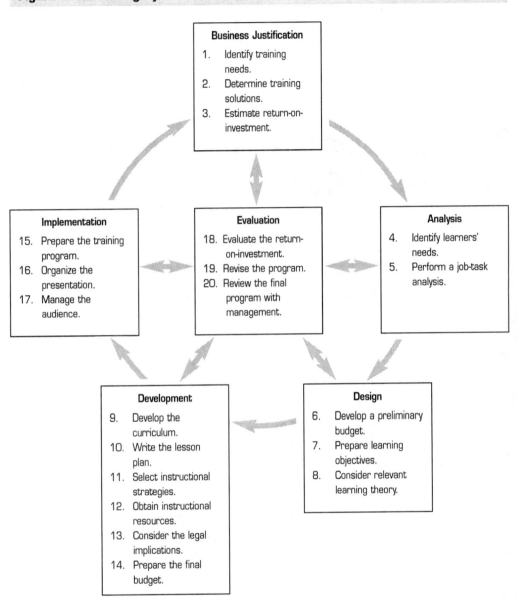

The model addresses three questions critical to any training program developer:

▽ What content should I include?

▽ How should I teach and deliver the content?

▽ How can I ensure that the training is working (that is, that trainees learn the content)?

Steps of the Training System Model

The training system model has 20 steps. The steps in the business justification stage, chapter 6, are as follows:

1. **Identify training needs**. Conduct a preliminary needs analysis. Determine the kind of performance problems the organization is experiencing. Find out who thinks these are problems and why. Use observations, questionnaires, interviews, tests, work samples, and records to help identify the training need.

2. **Determine training solutions**. Training does not solve all performance problems, and you must first determine if training will solve the problem that management believes exists. Thorough analysis of the needs will help to determine if training is the solution to the performance deficiencies.

3. **Estimate return-on-investment (ROI)**. The process of measuring ROI should be simple, economical, credible, as well as theoretically sound, flexible, and applicable with all types of data, including hard data (such as output, quality, costs, and time) and soft data (such as job satisfaction, customer satisfaction, grievances, and complaints).

The analysis stage, chapter 7, has two steps:

4. **Identify learners' needs**. Collect data on the needs of individuals who are or will be performing the tasks. Production records, performance appraisals, supervisors, and employees can provide the information needed to identify learners' needs.

5. **Perform a job-task analysis**. Once it is determined that training will solve the performance problems, analyze all the tasks that make up performance for particular jobs.

The following steps are in the design stage, chapter 8:

6. **Develop a preliminary budget**. Estimate the costs to decide whether to design or buy a training program.

7. **Prepare learning objectives**. Objectives, specified statements of what learners will do or know upon completion of the training, and help to define the content of the training program and ensure that the tasks required to perform are included in the program.

8. **Consider relevant learning theory**. Different theories explain how people learn, which occurs internally and can be inferred.

The development stage, chapter 9, has the following steps:

9. **Develop the curriculum.** The written documents should reflect the interaction of content, sequence, instructor's experience, learners' experience, and organization's expectations.

10. **Write the lesson plan.** Include in the plan the learning objective, content, instructor and learner activities, test items, and enabling knowledge.

11. **Select instructional strategies.** Strategies range from audiovisual equipment to a variety of group learning techniques. The lesson plan may need to be revised after selecting instructional strategies.

12. **Obtain instructional resources.** After completing the first draft of the training program, designers must make plans for the physical, financial, and human resources needed to conduct the program.

13. **Consider the legal implications.** Before pursuing the training in earnest, designers must check for possible violations of the law that the training program might create. These include copyright infringement and equal employment opportunity laws.

14. **Prepare the final budget.** The final budget is a complete estimate of training costs that is presented to management.

Implementation, chapter 10, has three steps:

15. **Prepare the training program.** Organize the content of the learning module. Learn about the audience and venue, and select the materials and format.

16. **Organize the presentation.** Plan your presentation, choosing to follow the theory or skill session model and writing the body, conclusion, and introduction. Select the method of delivery, including the visual aids.

17. **Manage the audience.** Watch the learners' reactions, and gauge their interest as you speak. Modify your presentation to be sure they remain in tune with you.

The final stage, chapter 11, evaluation, has the following steps:

18. **Evaluate the return-on-investment.** Has the training improved performance such that the organization's overall economic picture has improved? Measures such as sales and absenteeism can be tied to training.

19. **Revise the program.** Throughout the training program, obtain feedback to refine the program to best meet the learners' and organization's needs.

20. **Review the final program with management.** Management support must follow through well after learners complete the training program to ensure that the training had the desired results.

Although each chapter is self-contained and is designed to provide specific skills and techniques, as dictated by the 20-step training system model, in practice a number of questions and needs do arise with the development of a training. The tool kit, part III of this book, provides tools and techniques that respond to frequently asked questions and to tool needs. A review of the tool kit can add competence to your practice.

Summary

This chapter presents the 20-step training system model that will guide you through the various stages of designing and developing your training program. The steps are sequential and start with the critical first step of defining the training need. Once you have developed a needs statement, you have established a clear focus for building your training.

Check-Up Exercise

1. What is the initial, critical step you must take to begin the training design and development process?
2. How many steps are involved in the multistep training system model?
3. What is the rationale for using a structured design process for creating your training program?

▼ 6

Business Justification

The first step in designing a training program is to determine the business justification behind the training request and the implications of conducting, or not conducting, the training program. Managers use results of the business justification to

▽ decide whether to provide the training

▽ allocate resources

▽ prioritize a training program for scheduling purposes.

Businesses, business units, organizations, and associations all are concerned with leadership and motivation, though to different degrees. To best appeal to businesses that think that training will solve a performance problem, trainers should embody the following leadership qualities:

▽ Set a good example.

▽ Seek and take on new challenges.

▽ Be courageous in facing the unknown.

▽ Demonstrate resourcefulness when confronting and solving problems.

▽ Show concern for trainees' and organizations' well-being and success.

The ultimate criterion of leadership is the ability to inspire these same qualities in others to motivate changes in their behavior directed toward achieving specific goals. Trainers who demonstrate leadership traits are attractive to management. Businesses look for these kinds of qualities in their employees. Presenting yourself as a leader is a key element behind business justification for training.

Leadership, though an abstraction, can be recognized in others. People can learn leadership by using others as role models and by attending effective training programs.

As a trainer, you more than likely will be asked to develop a training program that solves a performance gap. The training you give to fill that gap should embody characteristics of leadership. By incorporating leadership qualities, you provide an environment in which employees are motivated to take on the challenge of applying what they learn.

If employees emerge from training with a sense that through the training the organization has sought to increase their well-being, the employees are likely to feel more committed to the organization's well-being. This return to the organization is definitely a business justification for training.

Employees can be confident about their abilities to perform on the job without being motivated to improve their performance. A properly designed and implemented training program will instill confidence and motivation in the people you train. Training that is based on a specific context and on techniques specific to the workplace will demonstrate that change is not only possible but also desirable and, thus, will be a step toward motivating employees to change.

As a trainer, you can help the organization determine if a business justification for the training exists by conducting performance and business analyses.

Identify Training Needs

A performance analysis is a process for determining if a training need or opportunity exists. Performance is defined as the achievement of effective outcomes from productive work. A performance need might be to provide training to address a gap in actual performance versus ideal performance. To identify performance needs, the client has to define ideal performance, and the consultant should be prepared to conduct a performance analysis for the client. During the course of a performance analysis, you must answer the following questions:

- Who is the client?
- What is the problem or need?
- What are the reasons for the problem or need?
- Why is the request being made now?
- What performance enhancement or deficiency is the training intended to address?
- What is the value or worth of the problem or need?
- Are there any red flags (for example, internal politics) that you need to consider?
- Who is the target population?
- What are the alternative ways in which the problem or need could be addressed?

Present the performance analysis summary containing the following information as a written report or an oral presentation:

- need identification
- reasons the need arose
- worth of the need or cost of not addressing it
- alternative actions available to address the need
- description of the target population
- explanation of how training can address the need
- description of the client's training objectives
- overview of tasks, skills, or knowledge, or combination of them, to be covered
- red flags or other training concerns to be considered.

Determine Training Solutions

A business analysis is a process for determining the return to the organization of investing in the training program. A business need might be in the area of improving productivity, managing and responding to the market competition, or introducing new processes or procedures required for improved business performance. The business analysis should address the following questions:

- What consequences will the training have on the organization's performance?
- Why is training perceived to be the solution?
- What are the clients' training objectives?
- What tasks, skills, or knowledge will the training program content cover?
- What alternative ways could the organization address the training problem or need?
- How would each of the alternatives enhance the organization's business strategy?
- How much does each alternative cost (in total resources required)?
- Which is the preferred alternative (with rationale)?
- What is the anticipated level of client commitment?
- What roles and responsibilities will each member of the training project team have?
- Are the required resources available from within the organization?
- Are the required resources available from outside the organization?
- Are there any constraints that will affect planning, preparing, or conducting?
- Are there any nontraining issues that might affect the program's progress?

Present the business analysis summary as a written report or an oral presentation. This analysis prepares the client for the training project agreement. The business analysis summary should cover the following issues:

- implications for the organization
- what the consequence would be on the organization's performance if the training were conducted or were not conducted
- alternative methods by which the training department can meet the training need
- costs of each alternative
- how each alternative might enhance the organization's business strategy
- preferred alternative with rationale
- organization-related constraints affecting the training program's design, development, or delivery
- client-related constraints affecting the training program's design or development
- implications for the training unit
- anticipated level of client commitment and support
- roles and responsibilities of all training program team members
- resources required and their availability
- nontraining issues that might affect the training program's progress.

You should draw your recommendations and conclusions from the performance and business analyses.

Estimate Return-on-Investment

The final aspect of the business justification involves preparing a brief training project agreement, as shown in figure 6-1. The purpose of the agreement is to ensure that the client understands exactly what training program will be provided.

The training project agreement should accomplish the following:

- describe the training program
- define preliminary objectives
- provide timelines for project completion
- list resources required
- identify any program limitations or constraints.

Budget allocations should be made after all parties involved have signed the agreement.

Figure 6-1. Training project agreement.

Project Name _____

Project Manager _____

Client Project Manager _____

Sponsor_____

Overview

Description of Training Project_____

_____

_____

Description of Preliminary Objectives_____

_____

_____

Work Plan

Project Start_____ Printer Materials Review_____ Pilot Test _____

Course Outline Review_____ Dry Run/Test _____ Course Release _____

Internal Resources Required (Who? When?) _____

_____

Externa Resources Required _____

Limitation or Constraints _____

_____

Sales Guide and Software Availability_____

_____

Assumptions and Contingencies _____

_____

_____   _____   _____
Project Manager Signature   Sponsor Signature   Client Signature

_____   _____   _____
Date   Date   Date

Summary

This chapter discusses the need for conducting a needs analysis. There are two basic needs that you must consider in developing training: a performance need and a business need. Once you determine the type of need, your next step is to share your analysis with your client so that you both recognize a mutual need and agree on the process for managing the defined need; this is where you develop your training project agreement.

Check-Up Exercise

1. What is meant by a performance need, and what is an example of a performance need?
2. What is meant by a business need, and what is an example of a business need?
3. What are the vital components of the training project agreement?

Analysis

After completing the business justification checkpoints process and obtaining a signed client training project agreement, you are ready to begin the second stage of the training system model, a needs analysis, also called the training needs assessment. A needs analysis is a systematic process of discovery to support change through training.

The needs analysis is the second stage and is the most critical step in the training system model because the information collected (using a combination of needs analysis tools) helps you to define the specific gaps that exist between current and desired organizational and individual performance. During the needs analysis process, you will identify opportunities, problems, or other issues to determine if there is a need for training.

This second stage in the training system model examines the context of a particular job, the skills required for performing the job, and the on-the-job knowledge required before you design training. An error in the analysis step can result in designing an unsuccessful training program. Although organizations operate differently and training varies with jobs and tasks, research shows that successful training initiatives have six common features:

1. **Management commitment.** Involving management early in the needs analysis process benefits everyone. Management is often the driving force behind a needs analysis. Remember to obtain management's support before beginning an analysis. By conducting a needs analysis in an environment that fosters mutual respect and honesty, you give yourself every advantage for reaching an agreement with management about the outcome of the analysis.

2. **Rationale for training**. It will save time and money to determine if training is appropriate. Providing a training simply because management requests or requires it does not guarantee success. You must decide if the issue under discussion calls for training. You must also establish

   ▼ how the proposed training affects the proposed audience
   ▼ acceptance from the likely audience, supervisors, and management
   ▼ training's effect on the entire organization.

3. **Questions that guide the process**. Defining the problem clearly is critical to developing a successful training. Answers to these questions help to define the area of need:

   ▼ Why do or don't people perform?
   ▼ What performance is desired?

4. **Factors that influence the process**. Trainers should examine knowledge, skills, and attitudes in the analysis. The work environment is an important factor in the process, so, too, is examining in detail individuals' skills, knowledge, and attitudes about their tasks, jobs, boss, and organization. Together, these factors influence your decision about whether to provide a training. They show that the problem has to do with an environmental problem (poor lighting, for example) or that it is the result of unrealistic deadlines, not inefficient training.

5. **Types of trainings**. Trainers should differentiate between the two types of solutions:

   ▼ training, which teaches an immediate job skill
   ▼ education, which provides theories, content, and knowledge to be applied in the future.

6. **Performance standards and criteria**. Establishing standards of excellence and using them as performance criteria are basic to operating an organization. Use the following indicators to measure individual and organizational performance:

   ▼ What should and does the organization consider baseline skills?
   ▼ What is the group intelligence of the individuals, groups, departments, and organization?
   ▼ What behaviors and attitudes exist?

Identify Learners' Needs

Learners' needs, which relate to performance, are organized into two types of needs: micro and macro. A micro need is one that exists for one person or for a small population. A macro need is one that exists for a large group of employees, frequently for the entire population with the same job classifications. You must consider both types of needs during the analysis stage. Some typical micro needs are as follows (Laird, 1985):

▽ New employees need to understand what is expected on the job.

▽ A three-person unit is expected to know how to operate newly installed microcomputers.

▽ A supervisor is having problems managing time.

Examples of macro needs are as follows:

▽ All employees need orientation when the company opens a new building.

▽ All employees are expected to be able to use a newly installed, company-wide computer system.

▽ All first-line supervisors are required to initiate performance appraisal discussions in their units.

Perform a Job-Task Analysis

To identify the topic to be presented in your training, first analyze skills required to perform the job. You begin your analysis by gathering enough information to develop a statement of the problem behavior. After you have gathered your information, proceed to investigating the situation, analyzing the causes, and reporting your fact-gathering results to management to gain permission to design and develop your training program. Let's consider each of the four steps.

Step 1: Surveillance

Once you receive the request to provide the training, scan the organization to determine if there is an organizational need and if the performance gap can be addressed with training. During this step, your focus is to determine if a training is required. Use the following six questions to help you to determine the nature of the problem:

1. Why this issue?
2. Whose need is it, and who is involved?
3. What is the issue?
4. When did this issue become a need?
5. Where did the issue begin?
6. What is the best way to solve this issue?

Next, you will need to arrange a meeting with the client. The goal of this meeting is to clearly define the training issue and agree on an outcome for the training.

Before you attend the initial client meeting, complete the premeeting guide, shown in figure 7-1, and the following:

- identify other staff, if any, who should attend
- prepare a questionnaire to record data
- explain the next steps in the process.

Figure 7-1. Example of a premeeting guide.

Needs Assessment Client Meeting #1: Premeeting Information

Date: _____

Place: _____

Time: _____

Contact: _____

Position: _____

Training issue(s): _____

_____

Guiding questions or topics: _____

_____

Next steps: _____

_____

During your meeting you should use the protocol, which appears in figure 7-2, to guide the discussion and document the training need as well as the following:

- define the task
- agree on the need and training outcome
- establish shared responsibility
- identify a contact person for the report
- obtain commitment to proceed.

After the meeting, write the client a summary memo. This summary should be sent to the client along with a request for a written commitment to continue the needs analysis. Additional information to include in the commitment letter should be a restatement of the agreed-upon allocation of resources, a list of the training

Figure 7-2. Example of a meeting guide.

Needs Assessment Client Meeting #1: Meeting Guidelines	
About the target task	**Responses**
Organization's performance standards	
Work conditions	
Supervisor's performance expectations	
About the participants	**Responses**
Stated training need(s)	
Current performance level(s)	
Current level(s) of knowledge	
Attitudes toward task	
Attitudes toward training	
About the training session	**Responses**
Timeframe for planning	
Stakeholders	
Conditions under which training will be conducted	
Available resources (e.g., materials, tools)	
Instructor's skills	

course objectives and outcomes, and a projected project timeline outlining all the steps required for the analysis process. Figure 7-3 is an example of a client summary memorandum.

Once you have completed the premeeting and received the go-ahead from the client, your project should officially begin. The next task is to decide what information to collect, which audience to survey, and which tools to use to collect and analyze the data.

There are two kinds of data to collect: hard and soft. Hard data is the factual and objective information that comes from reports and accounting records. Soft data is the opinions and other subjective information that comes from group discussions, interviews, and questionnaires. Table 7-1 lists the advantages and disadvantages of key hard data sources.

Figure 7-3. Example of a client summary memorandum.

Memorandum

To: Client

From: Trainer or facilitator

Date: January 2, 20xx

Subject: Needs assessment client meeting

1. Statement of the Problem
   Write a clear statement describing the assessment and training outcomes mutually agreed upon during the meeting.

2. Description of Tasks
   Define the tasks you perceived to be involved in the needs assessment process.

3. Summary of Analysis
   Summarize the information about the target tasks, the participants, and the training situation that would be informative to help management make a commitment to the process and the proposed training outcome.

4. Proposed Plan
   Present your plan for conducting the assessment including tasks, timeline, and project budget.

5. Request for Management's Commitment
   Request the client's written commitment to the project.

Table 7-1. Comparison of key hard data sources.

Method	Description	Advantage	Disadvantage
Human resource records	Provide causes regarding performance problems and training issues	Objective	Time-consuming
Accident and safety reports	Reveal clusters of issue types by department and position	Quantitative	Do not necessarily document causes
Grievance filings and turnover rates	State problem with employee or immediate supervisor	Documentation	Issues may be related to policy rather than to training
Performance evaluation and merit ratings	Measure analysis of employees on absolute and relative bases	Document skills and employee progress	Subjective information
Production statistics	Identify numerical results of output and itemized costs of doing business	Quantitative	Do not always provide a complete picture

Step 2: Investigation

Once you have gathered your information in step 1, you should organize it, review it, and decide the type of additional information you need. Once you have completed this phase, you can select the data collection method you will use and gather further data.

During the investigation, you are conducting research to determine whether a lack of training or some other organizational deficiency is causing the performance problem. Use the following questions to help establish some investigative parameters:

▼ What results does the organization obtain?
▼ How do these results compare with the organization's key objectives?
▼ What contribution does the training department need to make to meet the organization's key objectives?
▼ What method do you currently use to set priorities and justify training targets?
▼ How do you measure training results?

Data Collection

The problem to be addressed will guide your method for collecting data and the type of data you will collect. You should select from questionnaires, interviews (one-on-one, telephone, or focus groups), observations, precourse assignments, documentation, job descriptions, and policies and procedures.

As you collect data, remember that before solving any problem, you must clearly define the situation. Some tips for doing so follow:

▼ Ask who, what, where, why, when, and how questions.

▼ Develop a clear and concise problem statement.

▼ Separate facts from opinions.

▼ Document causes of the problem.

▼ Identify feelings about the problem.

▼ Determine who is involved and why.

▼ Formulate a resolution based on facts.

Figure 7-4. Example of client commitment letter.

XYZ Company
1000 The Street
City, State, Zip Code
(Area Code) Phone Number

February 2, 20xx

Ms. Dew Wright
Human Resources Director
XYZ Company
1234 The Street
City, State, Zip Code

Dear Ms. Wright:

As president of XYZ Company, I hereby fully support the project's objectives and proposed training outcomes, as stated in your January 25 summary memorandum. Concomitant with this commitment is the agreed upon availability of resources as requested.

With all best wishes for success.

Sincerely yours,

Philip Phillips
President

Obtain management's buy-in before you proceed. Make sure you have received a written response of management's commitment to the project. The commitment letter in figure 7-4 provides an example.

Determine skills, knowledge, and attitudes. In some circumstances, the issue that management identified may not be a training problem. So as not to waste training time, money, and other resources, you need to review the job and the related tasks, along with the skills, knowledge, and attitudes required for performance to determine if they relate to a training problem. Explore the following factors that cause performance problems:

▼ **Lack of skills and knowledge to do the job.** Can employees do the job tasks needed to meet the performance goals? If the answer is yes, there is no training problem and some other solution should be considered.

▼ **Lack of specific standards or job expectations.** Do employees know and understand their performance expectations?

▼ **Lack of feedback.** Do employees receive feedback about their performance?

▼ **Lack of necessary resources to perform.** Do employees have everything they need to perform?

▼ **Lack of appropriate consequences for performance.** Do employees receive appropriate incentives to perform adequately?

The recommendation for solving the problem may comprise several solutions, often involving training and some organizational solution. When a training deficit exists, further analysis is needed to determine the scope of a training.

Through interviews with people who want training conducted, complete figure 7-5 to acquire an analysis of the people who are likely to need the training. You may conduct several pretraining interviews for one program, speaking with several supervisors and potential participants. You may then complete several audience profiles, according to the number of people you interview, which you would then integrate into one form.

There are four factors to consider when analyzing your training audience: education, work experience, previous training, and implementation. On the basis of your audience analysis, you may propose that the training manager and finance manager attend a one-day train-the-trainer workshop.

Also, included in the audience analysis is an analysis of the current job. Have conversational interviews with people doing the job as well as with supervisors, using table 7-2 as a guide. The profile forms the structure of the interview. The results of the two forms will help you make choices about the language, course material, instructor, and location you will use.

Figure 7-5. Sample audience analysis profile.

Area	Questions	Findings
Education	Range of school experience	
	Native language	
	Average reading level	
Work Experience	Existing skills or knowledge related to proposed training	
	Variation of work experience levels	
Training	Motivation	
	Recent training experience	
	Effect on current job	
	Degree of accountability	
Delivery	Number of people to be trained	
	Location of people to be trained	

A job analysis will determine where the training issue really exists. Jobs consist of major functional areas, typically three or four. The job of senior acquisitions editor in book publishing, for example, has three main functions: to identify people who might become authors, to coordinate the production of manuscripts, and to conduct book sales. Under each of the areas are tasks. The function of coordinating manuscript production, for example, includes preparation of manuscripts for production, which includes checking for a copyeditor's comments and coordinating those comments with an author's responses.

In conducting a job analysis, you must identify enabling knowledge as well as functional areas, tasks, and performance elements. The enabling knowledge for acquisitions editors who coordinate editors' comments with authors' responses is an understanding

Table 7-2. Sample job analysis profile.

Job Title of Training: _____	
Functional Responsibilities	**Tasks Involved in Each**
Write 30-minute training module	Define objectives. Develop topical outline. Decide on instructional strategies. Produce course works.
Evaluate 30-minute training	Determine level of education. Include test items in design. Determine methods of data collection, analysis, and report.

of editors' terminology. A job analysis that breaks down the areas of a job assists you and course designers who are trying to determine a training need, say for editors, so course designers won't subject editors to trying on everything about their job.

One of your responsibilities is to compile a list of needs and ideas for training activities. Ideas for the list may come from several channels (for example, a formal needs analysis, a request from a specific unit, a request for training on some newly installed equipment, company literature, and observation of industry trends).

When collecting data, it is helpful to keep an annotated list of the material you keep in your files so you can readily respond to questions about potential training needs. The list also can help you monitor each issue to see where training is necessary. Table 7-3 shows an annotated list of files. The column on the left specifies the training issue, the middle column describes the current situation, and the column on the right describes the ideal situation. This is one way to organize information that comes to you through memorandums, newsletters, and other reports.

Continually add data and information to your list of files. By storing information and related data in this list whenever a training or performance issue arises, you will have some background information.

When a performance problem exists or an organizational need surfaces, the first thought that pops into people's heads is to train the problem away. However, solutions other than training should be considered. Before thinking about the type of training program, remember that you must determine if training is appropriate.

Table 7-3. Sample list of files.

Area	What Is Happening?	What Should Be Happening?
Organization's mission and objectives • Performance standards • Budget targets • Job descriptions • Production • Performance appraisals	Write guidelines. Be specific.	Be specific.
Rate of • Labor turnover • Absenteeism • Accidents • Disciplinary actions		
Costs • Labor • Materials • Overtime • Economic predictions • Technical development • Legal issues		

If you think training is needed, use the audience analysis profile and the problem analysis profile, as shown in figure 7-6, to establish the need for a training and to help you develop the content. Observe, interview, and analyze employees with the same or similar jobs, and integrate your findings into one form. This helps you to see where a problem lies, how big it is, whether employees have the skills, and who owns the problem. Without collecting and organizing this data, you would find it difficult to match your training to the participants' needs.

There are other good reasons to conduct a needs analysis before developing a training program. When trainers design training activities, they should obtain case material directly from the workplace or participants' personal situations. Armed with this information, they can base their designs on real issues that participants face, rather than on simulated material.

Figure 7-6. Sample problem analysis profile.

Performance Area	Accounts receivable
Performance Goal	All reps should exhibit proficiency. Use upgrades for coding billings.
Current Performance	Thirty percent of staff exhibit appropriate competency; 50 percent to be trained and tested.
Gap Between Goal and Performance	Fifty percent to be trained. All located outside headquarters in satellite offices.

Causes	Findings
Do employees have the skills and knowledge to meet the performance goals?	No, only 50 percent at headquarters
Do employees know the performance standards or expectations?	Yes, announced in bulletin
Do employees receive feedback about their performance?	Yes
Do employees have the necessary resources to perform?	Yes, will provide required training
Do employees receive appropriate incentives to perform?	Yes, profit sharing per group performance

Source: Adapted from S.V. Steadman, "Learning to Select a Needs Assessment Strategy," *Training and Development Journal* (Alexandria, VA: ASTD, 1980).

How to Collect Information

As trainers think about the kind of information that would be useful, they should consider asking the potential participants to identify their needs. By going directly to the participants for the information prior to the training, trainers give the participants roles in designing and developing their own program. Involvement at this early stage also enables trainers to develop a relationship with the participants and their supervisors and managers. Because the supervisors and managers appreciate your involvement, they are likely to be receptive to the program, which increases the likelihood of its success.

There are advantages and disadvantages of collecting information by observation and questionnaires, as outlined in table 7-4. If you cannot collect information directly from each person in your target audience, consider the following two options:

1. Send a questionnaire to participants before meeting them. This provides you with an opportunity to tell them about yourself and your plans for the upcoming program, and it helps you to learn about them.

2. Phone or visit some or all the participants for an assessment interview. This option provides the opportunity for face-to-face interaction and minimizes awkward feelings when you meet in the classroom at the start of the program.

There are three primary sources of training needs: the people, the job, and the organization, as table 7-5 shows. A source internal to the organization means that someone or something within your organization brings the problem or issue to your attention. A source external to the organization means that a person, place, or thing not within your organization brings the problem or issue to your attention. Often the first sign that training might be needed surfaces as a specific problem within one of the three primary sources. You then need to define the problem in more depth. You must decide if the problem is

- performance related
- short- or long-term
- new or recurring
- affecting few or many employees
- urgent, important, or unimportant.

By defining the problem, you are able to target it and prioritize your response. Generally, if the problem affects a few people, deal with the few. Find out what's going on, and determine what should be going on. Determine if the issue is urgent and to whom it is urgent. Find out how the stakeholders want it resolved and when. If it doesn't seem urgent, determine who the stakeholders are and how they want the issue resolved.

Table 7-4. Advantages and disadvantages of observations and questionnaires.

Observations	Advantages	Disadvantages
• Can be as technical as time-motion studies or as functionally or behaviorally specific as observing a new board or staff member interacting during a meeting • May be as unstructured as walking through an agency's offices on the lookout for evidence of communication barriers • Can be used normatively to distinguish between effective and ineffective behaviors, organizational structures, or process	• Minimize interruption of routine work flow or group activity • Generate factual data, highly relevant to the situation where response to identified training needs and interests will have an effect • Provide important comparison checks between the observer's and the respondent's inferences (when combined with a feedback step)	• Require a highly skilled observer with both process and content knowledge (unlike an interviewer who needs, for the most part, only process skills) • Carry limitations because able to collect data only within the work setting (flip side of the first advantage)
Questionnaires	**Advantages**	**Disadvantages**
• May be surveys or polls of a random or stratified sample of respondents, or an enumeration of an entire population • Can use a variety of question formats: open ended, projective, forced choice, priority ranking • Can take alternative forms such as rating scales, either redesigned or self-generated by one or more respondents • May be self-administered (by mail) under controlled or uncontrolled conditions or may require the presence of an interpreter or assistant	• Reach a large number of people in a short time • Are relatively inexpensive • Provide opportunity for expressing self without fear of embarrassment • Yield data that can be easily summarized and reported	• Make little provision for free expression of unanticipated responses • Require substantial time (and technical skills, especially in survey model) for developing effective instruments • Are of limited utility in getting at causes or problems or possible solutions • Suffer low return rates (mailed), grudging responses, or unintended or inappropriate respondents

Source: Adapted from S.V. Steadman, "Learning to Select a Needs Assessment Strategy," *Training and Development Journal* (Alexandria, VA: ASTD, 1980).

Table 7-5. Sources of training needs.

Source	Internal to Organization	External to Organization
People	• Potential trainers • Supervisors • Upper-level managers	• Trainers in other organizations • Outside consultants
Job	• Personnel changes (e.g., new hires, promotions) • Job task changes • Changes in performance standards • Equipment changes • Analyses of efficiency indexes (e.g., waste, downtime, repairs, quality control)	• Professional associations • Outside consultants • Government regulations
Organization	• Changes in the organization's mission • Mergers and acquisitions • Change in organizational structure • New products and services • Analysis of organizational climate (e.g., grievances, absenteeism, turnover, accidents)	• Government regulations and legislative mandate • Outside consultants • Pressure from outside competition • Environmental pressure (e.g., political, economic, demographic, technical)

Source: R. Caffarella, *Program Development and Evaluation Resource Book for Trainers* (New York: John Wiley, 1988).

If the problem is short term, you might rectify it by developing a mechanism that uses a job aid, or you might meet with a group of people involved with it. If the problem is new or recurring, you might have to devote training resources to investigate it.

Is training appropriate? Use the data summary sheet in figure 7-7 to guide your decision about the appropriateness of training. When there is no time to conduct an analysis, do the following:

▼ Phone a contact person who is familiar with the participants. Use the audience analysis and the problem analysis profile sheets.

▼ Introduce yourself and ask participants some key questions. Trust the responses to be representative, and treat them as if they were a sample of the large group. Or ask a contact person to schedule a phone interview for you.

▼ Ensure that you receive relevant materials (such as surveys, meeting notes, records).

▼ Obtain opinions and impressions from other trainers who have worked with the training group.

▼ Talk to participants who arrive early, and obtain whatever information you can.

▼ Design some activities at the beginning of the program to enable you to assess the group.

▼ If you conducted some front-end analysis and designed your program on the basis of your analysis results, you should be able to make final adjustments before the training meeting begins.

Step 3: Analysis

In this step you will take all the information you collected through your investigation and organize it in various ways to analyze the information. Several analytical techniques exist. Before beginning to undertake the rigors of analysis, you should review the data summary sheet and record the information according to the source, required skill set, and the type of need (educational or training), and you should establish priorities. Use the data summary sheet organizer in figure 7-8 to sort the information collected from the data summary sheets.

Figure 7-7. Data summary sheet.

1. Outline the problem or need in the organization for which you believe a training might be appropriate. Be as specific as possible.

2. Determine whether the need or problem you have identified is performance related and why or why not. If the need or problem is related to performance, go to number 3. If the need or problem is not related to performance, go to number 5.

3. Is this a macro or micro problem? What action are you suggesting?

4. Classify the need or problem you have identified as something your employees (check one):

   a. Do not know (lack of knowledge)...............□

   b. Cannot do (lack of skill)...........................□

   c. Can do, but aren't motivated to do ....□

5. Identify possible solutions to the problem or need other than training. List these alternatives.

Figure 7-8. Data summary sheet organizer.

Source	Evidence of Need	Skills Sets	Education or Training	Priority
Organization	Satellite offices	Coding	Upgrade coding procedure	High
People	Finance staff in billing office of satellite	Analyzing and critical thinking		
Job	Accounts or billing			

In recording information about the job, break down a job or function into tasks to pinpoint where the training or performance need exists. Several methods are available to help you identify the job tasks. Review job literature, observe job performance, and question people on the job.

At this point, you will have broken down the functional responsibilities into tasks. Validate the job analysis with an advisory group made up of subject matter experts, management representatives, and client contacts to guarantee that the job analysis matches the job. Using table 7-6, ask the advisory group to help select the key functions and tasks that will be the focus of your training course. It is often necessary to select key tasks because there is not enough time to prepare training for everything that was uncovered in a job analysis.

Present Findings

There are several ways to present findings: check sheets, line graphs, and Pareto charts. Check sheets are easy to design and use. As table 7-7 shows, check sheets use hash marks to show the frequency of events. A check sheet allows you to decide what events to record, determine the time period for the observation (for example, hours, days, months), and develop the format. Information from check sheets is easily transferable to a frequency graph.

A line graph displays trends in a particular activity over a specific time period. Use the line graph to identify changes as soon as they occur. By noting the change immediately, you can recommend taking prompt action.

Table 7-6. Sample job analysis questionnaire.

Task	How Frequently Do You Perform This Task?			Where Did You First Learn How to Perform This Task?				How Critical Is This Task to Your Job?			What Is the Best Way to Learn This Task?		
	Never	Sometimes	Often	On the Job	School	Training	Other	Very	Somewhat	Not Very	On the Job	Training	Other
1.													
2.													
3.													
4.													
5.													
6.													

Source: Author, 1995.

Table 7-7. Sample check sheet.

Delay	3	4	5	6	Total
Missing information	II	I	III	II	8
Policy changes/questions	₦	₦ II	IIII	₦ III	24
Input errors	₦ IIII	₦ ₦ III	₦ II	₦ IIII	38
Alerts/routing		I	II	I	4
Individual work habits	II	III	II	III	10
Total	18	25	18	23	84

A Pareto chart, as shown in figure 7-9, is a bar chart that displays the relative importance of events or needs. The most frequent events or greatest needs (the higher the numbers) appear to the left of the chart. The Pareto chart is similar to the check sheet in its ability to identify root causes of problems.

Take Action

Once the organization has developed a clear picture of the training priorities, the next step is to decide the best way to meet the needs. The organization has several options:

▼ Design, develop, and deliver the training program in-house.

▼ Contract with an outside consultant to design and develop the coursework for in-house delivery.

▼ Contract with an outside training facility to handle all aspects of the training.

▼ Purchase a commercial training program, and train in-house staff to teach the program.

Organizations without in-house training departments usually have to look outside for all but the most basic type of on-the-job training programs. For organizations that have internal training staff, the decision is more complex. Answers to the following questions can help narrow the choice:

▼ How often and to how many employees will the training program be offered?

▼ Do we have a content expert with credible delivery skills?

▼ Will the training program address a one-time need targeted to only a few employees, or will the program take place only a few times a year?

Figure 7-9. Sample Pareto chart.

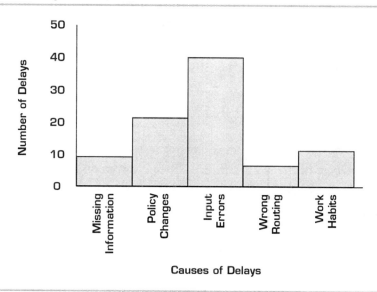

Causes of Delays

▼ Will training involve generic skills or a specific, technical need?

▼ Will the trainees be lower-level staff or upper-level managers?

▼ Will the content of the program involve proprietary or competitive information?

In thinking about the questions, consider the cost effectiveness of training. If training will be infrequent, it may be more cost effective to use an outside consultant. Alternatively, ongoing training needed by many employees may be more cost effective if developed and delivered in-house. When training involves technology, equipment, or skills unique to the organization and its jobs, in-house design and delivery may be the only option. For top management, a consultant's polished presentation and broad range of experience with other companies enhance the program's credibility. For lower-level positions, trainees may view a program as more relevant and credible if it is developed and delivered by someone familiar with day-to-day problems. If the content of the training program is proprietary, developing and delivering the program in-house is preferred.

Negotiate Training Objectives

Training program objectives should be clearly stated to ensure they include those critical activities or performance issues that will be accepted as evidence that the participants learned something. Training should follow the sequence of the objectives so that learning occurs in a logical progression.

There are two types of objectives—terminal and enabling:

▼ Terminal objectives describe what a training program participant will be able to do at the end of the training program and under what conditions and at what level of competence the participant must perform. Terminal objectives are the cornerstone of a training program because training program developers, instructors, participants, clients, and evaluators all use them.

▼ Enabling objectives flow from the major task statements (for example, output, nature of the organization). These types of objectives represent the basic skills, knowledge, and attitudes that must be learned before meeting the course objective.

Design Training and Course Module

The instructional specifications serve as a blueprint for program development. They are guidelines for content, timing of presentation of ideas, and reasons the content is included. The completed program can then be compared to the blueprint when the training course is evaluated.

Specifying instructional content is a joint effort by training and subject matter experts. In this part of the analysis, the critical content of the modules is defined systematically. The instructional strategy used when introducing the content, determining appropriate learning techniques, providing opportunities for practice, and determining the appropriate media forms must be clearly defined as well. All media selected should have a definite purpose. Instructional specifications include the following:

▼ module name
▼ introduction
  — content summary
  — utility
  — importance
▼ sequence of topics and activities
  — flow
  — transitions
  — links
▼ objectives
  — special teaching point
  — media requirements
  — testing requirement
  — learner/trainer activities.

Continue Ongoing Needs Analysis

An effective training department must continually plan, design, deliver, and assess its training. The following steps provide a useful strategy:

▼ Step 1: Assess ongoing training. What training do employees need? What new skills will the organization need in the future? Conduct an annual needs survey. Track the identified needs, and concentrate on those first by developing a six-month or yearlong training agenda. Some typical categories of training topics include

— health and safety topics

— sales and customer service training

— clerical, technical, specialized, interpersonal, or managerial skills

— professional development programs, such as career and personal development

— succession planning.

▼ Step 2: Design training programs. Determine the following for each training program you develop:

— course objectives

— test items

— instructional methods

— material content

— course and module design

— training program length

— method for identifying participants

— trainer and program management

— budget

— training announcement

— registration and confirmation process.

▼ Step 3: Design training course and sample course modules. Before beginning the training program, sell the program to employees and management. Meet with selected instructors to ensure the training goal is consistent with your design and instructional methodology. Check the materials, logistics, and evaluation mechanism.

▼ Step 4: Create the training report. Before beginning to design a training, describe clearly your training concept and secure management's approval.

▼ Step 5: Return to step one.

Choose Trainers

Organizations that choose to deliver training in-house must decide who should conduct the training sessions. Large organizations may have a fully qualified staff of training professionals who can handle most teaching assignments. Smaller organizations, however, will need to locate a qualified staff person or outside trainer to handle the assignment.

▼ *In-house personnel.* For many types of training, qualified course instructors can be found within the organization. Each executive, for instance, has expertise in a certain area, and most can make time to conduct at least one or two training sessions. Other potential instructors include supervisors and managers; human resource personnel, especially those with career counseling and similar experience; and professional employees, particularly ones who have had previous teaching experience.

▼ *Outside trainers.* Part- and full-time faculty at area colleges and universities are ideal candidates to recruit as trainers. Depending on the nature of the course, other outside professionals to consider as either instructors or guest speakers include consultants, lawyers, psychologists, systems analysts, or efficiency experts. Professional and trade associations as well as local chambers of commerce may be able to provide you with the names of experts who would be willing to make presentations.

Step 4: Reporting

This final step in conducting a needs analysis is your opportunity to present your work from the first three steps. By organizing the information from surveillance and investigation and discussing your interpretations from analysis, you can now succinctly and clearly convince management that the training you propose will solve the identified problem and respond to management's request. Communicating the results in writing and in a spoken presentation usually improves chances for success.

The training design report defines and documents findings of the needs analysis process and summarizes the problem statement, the analyses used to determine the training need, and the proposed module design. In the final report, discuss how your findings relate to the organization's overall strategy and goals and how the proposed change or training program will benefit the organization and the employees.

Training Design Report

Aimed at a wide audience, many of whom may not be familiar with the topic, and written in simple, clear language, a training design report summarizes the results of the investigation and analysis, communicates progress to key management, and provides the training manager with material for supervising each stage of the project. The following components make up a training design report:

- **Purpose of proposed course**. Describes the training problem, the training format, and the history of the problem within the organization. Keep this section to one paragraph.

- **Summary of analysis**. Summarizes the need. Defines clearly the performance gaps that the proposed training will address. Describes the audience. Explains the job, the tasks that make up that job, and the key performance elements needed to fulfill the job requirements. An extensive description is needed because the performance gap is probably located in a task, a performance element of the task, or a lack of misunderstanding of the knowledge the participants need to perform the task.

- **Scope of the course**. Establishes the format for the course. Presents an overview of the materials, the content, and the instructional strategies.

- **Learning objectives**. Presents the learning objective statements that will guide the course and the learning.

- **Test item strategy**. Describes how the participants will demonstrate mastery of the topic. Discusses how you will conduct the testing and why and what happens after the testing. For example, if the participants fail a test item, you should decide if the test item should be rewritten or determine if the training materials are problematic.

- **Course and module design**. Provides the instructional methods; the length of the course; and the training format, timing, and location.

- **Delivery strategy**. Outlines the instructional methods, the length of the course, the training format, the timing, and the location.

- **Evaluation or measurement tools**. Explains your evaluation mechanism and how you are going to measure the participants' reactions to the training, their learning (meaning the results of the test items), and their behavior (meaning how the concepts will be mastered).

Final Report

Again, using clear, concise language, a final report presents the results of all phases of the needs analysis. The report will identify performance gaps between the position in question and the function of the position. The final report includes the complete picture of what needs to be changed, how changes will be made, and how the organization and individuals will be affected by the changes. Think of the final report as the final sales presentation to all levels of the organization. The following components make up the final report:

▼ **Executive summary**. Answers the question, "If readers are too busy to look at the entire report, what's the least amount of information they need to make an informed decision?" This first section is critical. The executive summary should be short—one page is best.

▼ **Objectives of the needs analysis**. Provides the opportunity to explain in detail the objectives of the needs analysis. What information did you hope to learn in conducting a needs analysis of the organization or of a particular department?

▼ **Brief summary of findings**. Discusses optimal performance (what the organization hopes to achieve), actual performance (the organization's current level of performance), and how to bridge the gap between the two.

▼ **Proposed change or training project**. Explains the commitment involved. How much will the program cost? How long will it take to complete? How long will it be before we see results? Who will be involved? How will the program be implemented? What resources are needed for the program to succeed?

▼ **Data collection methods**. Explains why you collected the data you did and the process you used to analyze the data and information.

▼ **Expanded discussion of findings**. Discusses study results in detail. However, unless you have prepared the presentation for highly analytical thinkers, you may want to present findings in a descriptive form. You can include simple tables and graphs, but also describe the results in words. Save copies of the actual questionnaires for an appendix to the report.

▼ **Implications and analysis**. Discusses the implications of your results and relates the data to the organization's objectives.

▼ **Recommendations for future action**. Presents specific recommendations for future action. Recommendations should include at least the skills, knowledge, and attitudes required for a particular position, a training strategy (what a training program might look like, in other words, a module design in graphic form), and other issues you uncovered that management should resolve before proceeding with the proposed change or training program or concurrently with the program.

▼ **Appendixes of supporting data**. Includes relevant supporting data, such as sample surveys and other data collection methods, detailed analysis of the results, a cost breakdown, and a timeline of the proposed change.

It is critical that you know your audience when you are presenting your findings orally. As much as possible, learn about their values, attitudes, and needs. The presentation should focus on answering the question, "What's in it for me?"

Follow these tips when you work with PowerPoint presentations or overhead transparencies in presenting your report:

▼ Use few words per frame.

▼ Use pleasing and easy-to-see colors, such as blue as foreground or background, rather than yellow, which fades, or red, which is difficult to read.

▼ Use some type of bulleted list.

▼ Use graphics or images.

▼ Keep charts and graphs simple.

You, not the frames, are the show. The oral presentation reinforces the material provided in the written reports.

Summary

Analysis is a key element in the training process. For a successful training program, ensure that you do the following:

▼ Remember the six strategies for success—management commitment, rationale for training, questions that guide the process, factors that influence the process, types of trainings, and performance standards and criteria.

▼ Identify learners' needs.

▼ Follow the four-step needs analysis process—surveillance (scan the organization to determine if there is a need or performance gap); investigation (determine the type of data you need to guide your decision about a training and determine the data collection method); analysis (obtain a clear picture of the problem, the evidence, and the data sources to help determine the type of problem and determine the best source for training—using in-house personnel, hiring consultants, or purchasing a complete package); and reporting (present your findings to management).

▼ Consider time, need, timeliness, and cause and effect when conducting your needs analysis. Remember, your goal is to develop a well-defined problem statement during the surveillance step, identify the problem by gathering information in the investigation step, analyze the information collected, and report your findings.

Check-Up Exercise

1. What is the critical step in the training process?
2. What are the six strategies for success?
3. What are the four steps in the needs analysis process?

Design

The training needs analysis completed in chapter 7 provides needed information about the organization from the operational areas where problems exist. The information collected is considered the input of the analysis step. The output of the analysis step consists of identifying the training and nontraining needs and their priorities.

The nontraining needs that you have identified become the inputs to other functional areas, such as compensation, awards, or organizational development issues. The training needs become inputs to the next step in the process called design. The initial step in design is to develop training objectives and identify the factors needed in the training program to facilitate learning and its transfer back on the job.

Given the analysis that you have gone through, you have enough information to prepare a preliminary budget. This budget will help you decide if you are going to purchase a generic program from a vendor or if you are going to custom design the program.

Develop a Preliminary Budget

The basis for the budget is the amount of hours of design time, the size of the audience, and the frequency of the presentation. If the program would be for a small number of people, you could send them to training or have an expert provide training at your organization for a few hours or a day.

If at this stage it appears that you will be designing the program, you must take many factors into account. Some factors will apply at the outset. As the designer, you will determine others, and as you train, you will determine still others. In most cases, the information you collected during the analysis stage will help you in this process. If not, use your creativity to fill in the gaps.

After completing the needs analysis, you will know if the issue is a training problem and, if it is, what the trainees need to learn. The training need that you have identified needs to be translated into a well-defined training action statement called a training objective. The training objective establishes the trainee learning outcome, the design strategy, and the elements for the evaluation process.

Learning objectives are defined as models of learning theory. Once you have clarified the objectives and decided on which model of learning theory is relevant, you can select the content and organize the learning modules.

Prepare Learning Objectives

Learning objectives may be the most critical input in designing training. People are more likely to complete training successfully if they are told at the outset of the session what the goals of the training are.

When designing training, take a cue from textbook planners. The beginning of most textbook chapters lists the learning objectives for that chapter. More than likely, the chapter was designed around these learning objectives. This means that the author organized the content, including examples and exercises, in sequences that best match the learning objectives, just as trainers use the set of objectives for the session to determine and direct the design of the session.

Objectives are tools that point to the content and procedures that will lead to successful instruction, help you manage the actual instructional process, and help you prepare methods for finding out whether the instruction succeeded. Some objectives are useful, whereas others serve no purpose. A useful objective succeeds in communicating an instructional intent to the trainees and paints a picture of a successful learner. It pinpoints your intent and excludes other possible meanings.

Our language is full of fuzzy words that can be interpreted in a number of ways. Although it may be useful to use fuzzy words in some situations, it isn't useful in training. If you state the objectives using fuzzy words, you leave the training open to interpretations.

▼ ▼ ▼

When designing the training program, target these three outcomes:

- what the training will accomplish for the organization
- what the training will accomplish for the trainees
- how the accomplishments will be measured.

▲ ▲ ▲

When stating objectives, use terms that are not open to misunderstanding to ensure that people in a training program know what is expected of them at the completion of the program. For example, an objective that states, "At the end of this workshop, you will be able to install an XYZ window air conditioning unit without assistance," is more informative than one that says, "At the end of this workshop, you will know how to install an XYZ window air conditioning unit." Table 8-1 compares fuzzy words with specific words.

Table 8-1. Fuzzy vs. specific words.

Fuzzy Words	Specific Words
Know	Write
Understand	Recite
Appreciate	Identify
Grasp the significance of	Sort
Enjoy	Solve
Believe	Construct
Internalize	Build
	Compare
	Contrast

For objectives to communicate and be useful, they must have certain characteristics. All objectives must be specific, measurable, and observable. The format below includes three characteristics—performance, condition, criterion—each of which, when posed as a question, communicates an objective or behavioral intent. Table 8-2 shows how this format works.

- ▼ **Performance**. What should the learner be able to do? An objective always says what a learner is expected to do as a result of the training. The performance is always the verb.
- ▼ **Condition**. Under what conditions do you want the learner to be able to perform? An objective always describes the important conditions, if any, under which performance is to occur. The condition always refers to the resources.
- ▼ **Criterion**. How well must the learner perform? Whenever possible, an objective describes how well the learner must perform to be considered acceptable.

Most trainings are intended to accomplish a variety of goals. Usually trainers have some new information, a procedure, a policy, or a theory to impart to trainees. Trainers

Table 8-2. Characteristics of the objectives planning tool.

Objective	Performance	Condition	Criterion
Using the given equipment, the trainee must be able to execute three quarter-inch sutures within one minute.	execute three quarter-inch sutures	the given equipment	within one minute
Given the formal training report format, write a three- to five-page training needs analysis report covering all the report components that meets the trainer's specifications.	write a three- to five-page training needs analysis report	given the formal training report format	meets the trainer's specifications

often want trainees to develop skills in using that information on the job to solve problems, make decisions, and carry out tasks. Sometimes trainers are interested in changing attitudes and values or in increasing sensitivity or tolerance.

Articulating the training goals would not be so critical if trainers could pursue all of them in essentially the same way. However, research on learning indicates that different types of goals require different teaching methods and learning activities.

Identify Objectives

The success or effectiveness of the training you design relates directly to the instructional objectives. If a reason for the learning exists, then you must clearly specify the objectives. There are two strategies for communicating objectives: provide behavioral objectives and provide topical objectives.

Provide behavioral objectives that do the following:

▼ Delineate what trainees are expected to know when they begin the training.
▼ Specify the nature and quantity of new information to be provided by the training program.
▼ Specify the desired results (the behavior that is to occur once training has been completed successfully).

▼ Indicate the time and conditions needed to carry out the training program and implement the behavioral changes.

▼ Indicate how the behavioral change will be measured, including the circumstances under which the outcome will be measured along with a statement of minimum acceptable performance (how well or fast a task is to be performed).

▼ Include caveats, restrictions, and limitations related to any of the above.

Here is an example of a well-defined objective: Using the map reference guide, name correctly every item shown on each of the 20 blueprints in 20 minutes.

One example of a poorly stated objective is as follows: Understand the functions of all calculators after one lesson.

Topical objectives should tell participants what they are about to learn. An objective might say that participants will be able to use the new inventory system and have an overall knowledge of how the system functions.

Practice Objectives

People are more likely to accomplish the objectives if they are given opportunities to practice the behaviors identified in them. If trainees are to use the new information to make decisions, they need opportunities during the training course to practice decision making.

There are three types of practice:

▼ concentrated, in which practice takes place during a concentrated time period to increase the efficiency of learning new information, concepts, principles, or skills

▼ distributed, in which practice takes place over a period of time to increase retention

▼ varied, in which practice takes place in a variety of settings.

Write Specific Objectives

By writing specific behavioral objectives, you make it easier to measure what the trainees learn. To learn if the objective is specific, ask the following five questions:

1. Who is to perform the task?
2. What category of learning is involved?
3. What is the terminal behavior?
4. Under what conditions will the terminal behavior be demonstrated?
5. What level of proficiency is to be met to succeed?

Extensive educational research has identified a model of three major learning categories:

▼ **Skills (psychomotor).** Psychomotor ability is the actions that employees use in performing their jobs, such as writing and operating equipment. Skills can be observed and, therefore, are easily quantifiable.

▼ **Knowledge (cognitive).** Cognitive ability is what employees know in order to perform, such as the principles of accounting. Knowledge is not easily quantifiable.

▼ **Attitudes (affective).** Affective ability is what employees bring to the job in terms of feelings—how people feel about what they do and about the organization for which they are working affects their performance.

An objective written in the psychomotor domain will specify that trainees will develop a skill. It will require that trainees coordinate their brains with physical activity.

An objective written in the cognitive domain will state that the training is designed to enable trainees to know or understand something. After the session, trainees will be able to point the something out, describe the something, recognize the something, or define the something.

An objective in the affective domain will use verbs that connote feelings and emotions, such as respect, cooperate, and enjoy.

After delivering the training, you can evaluate the trainees' performance relative to your original objectives. Now, you must decide how you want to create the means for getting there—the design. Later, you can arrange to find out whether you arrived, as chapter 11 will explain.

If the training fails, the objectives may have been unclear or unrelated to on-the-job performance. Training may also fail because elements based on adult learning principles were missing or poorly integrated into the design.

Consider Relevant Learning Theory

Effective training requires understanding relevant learning theory and adult learning principles. The easiest way to understand the various learning theories is to define the differences among the various learning theories.

Learning is not directly observable, yet learning is something that almost everyone can experience. For example, people say, "I feel I know that now," or "I saw how that formula works," or "I know I can hear how different the sounds and letter accents are."

What influences learning? You are limited to observing the learner's behavior, and because learning is measured in terms of a relatively permanent change in behavior, this learning process becomes the operational definition for many learning theorists.

Cognitive versus Behaviorist Learning Theorists

Cognitive theorists insist that even though learning can be inferred from behavior, it is separate from the behavior itself. For example, you can memorize a phone number, use it, and then forget it, therefore suggesting no permanent change. So, from the cognitive theorist perspective, learning is defined as a relatively permanent change in thinking as a result of experience.

The behaviorist theorist's approach suggests that learning is controlled by the environment.

At first you might think the definition of learning may not seem to be important when designing training, yet these differences in the learning process can dictate different approaches to designing and implementing training. An obvious distinction that might affect your training is that the behaviorist approach suggests that the trainer controls learning by controlling the stimuli and consequences of that learner experience.

The cognitive approach suggests that learning is controlled by learners, meaning that learners come to training with their own set of goals and priorities; they process a set of cognitive structures for understanding their environment and how it works.

Table 8-3 offers a list elements that can influence your training design depending on the learning theory approach.

The adoption of one approach leads to implications for how training is conducted and the atmosphere of the training environment. Some training implications of

Table 8-3. Influential elements in a training.

Issue	Cognitive Approach	Behavioral Approach
Learner role	Active, self-directed	Passive, dependent
Trainer role	Facilitate, present	Direct, monitor
Training content	Problem or task oriented	Subject oriented
Learner motivation	Internally motivated	Externally motivated
Training climate	Relaxed, mutual trust	Formal, authority oriented
Training goals	Collaboratively developed	Developed by instructor
Training activities	Interactive, group	Directive, individual

cognitive and behaviorist learning theory should be considered in your design; look at the various training program elements that you can influence by the type of learning theory you choose for your design and implementation steps.

Both the cognitive and behaviorist approaches provide insight into the process of learning and furnish practical tools for increasing the effectiveness of training. Know and consider the theoretical differences, your training approach, and the various learning styles of your audience.

Learning theory describes how individuals learn. Much of what takes place during learning can be influenced by external events and learner goals and motivations, which make instruction possible. Learning, like eating, is one of the most fundamental processes of survival, yet as trainers, we sometimes complain that trainees don't pay attention, are disruptive, and generally demonstrate a resistance to the training. The first thing to think about when designing your training is resistance to learning. Most learning that occurs does not happen automatically or unconsciously; it is an activity trainees decide to do. Most trainees arrive at a training with an elaborate and highly integrated cognitive structure. They already know a lot about themselves, their work, and their organization. The objective of the training they are to attend is to change some part of that cognitive structure so that the trainees' performance will improve. Change creates anxiety for learners. One way to manage the trainees' anxiety is to ensure that your content design is organized around learning objectives and that the activities have been created to target all learner styles.

Learner Styles

There are no right or wrong ways to absorb new information. The methods by which people learn are complex. More than likely your trainees will be one of the following types of learner: confident, affective, transitional, integrated, or risk taking.

Confident Learners

Confident learners want to know why they are assigned particular tasks. A task assigned to confident learners must have a clear purpose. If they are given the opportunity, confident learners will set their own goals and may even help set direction for the training session. Confident learners like to be involved and consulted and will happily respond to a request to identify issues, problems, or themes on which they would like the training to focus. In some cases, trainers can use confident learners to help decide what content would be relevant and meaningful.

Confident learners sometimes prepare in advance for training sessions and may very well be irritated by trainers who progress too slowly, have less than well-defined objectives, or do not seek input from the trainees. Confident learners may be potential leaders and need opportunities for interactive learning. Group discussions, team projects, and shared experiences appeal to confident learners as do learning from peers and helping peers learn. Confident learners prefer training sessions that lead to specific goals. These learners may actually confront trainers whose programs or techniques appear inadequate, but they will not threaten well-prepared trainers.

Affective Learners

Affective learners like to know and feel that they are doing fine. Affective learners are influenced by their feelings. They want to feel an attachment to their trainers, and they expect the trainers to be experts who will explain, synthesize, and decrease the complexity of a subject. Affective learners want to be invited to participate and can be counted on for their patience, endurance, and loyalty when the path to reaching a learning goal might seem long and circuitous to others.

To best reach affective learners, trainers should do the following:

- Provide clearly written assignments or clearly defined exercises.
- Encourage enjoyable learning activities, such as interaction with other adults who value training.
- Specify particular reference books for further information.
- Recognize that these learners will strive to fulfill the trainer's reasonable and well-defined expectations.

Transitional Learners

Transitional learners are those who are being promoted or moving horizontally to a new job. These learners tend to focus more than others on the particular type of information they are learning and on how that learning will apply to their new situations. Transitional learners may be apprehensive about making job changes and may want to tell trainers either about the work experience or environment from which they are coming or about the work experience or environment to which they are moving. Transitional learners need to be reassured that they are fully capable of learning and succeeding. Trainers can do so by inviting these learners to discuss training objectives and techniques.

Transitional learners tend to see everything as potentially new and highly relevant. Many of them may not yet be familiar with all aspects of their new work environment. To best appeal to these learners, challenge them to learn. Transitional learners may not expect everything that is covered in the training session to have simple, obvious, and conclusive outcomes.

Integrated Learners

Integrated learners present a particularly interesting challenge to trainers because more often than not they establish peerlike relationships with trainers. Integrated learners are not satisfied merely to receive information; they want to do something with the information they receive. Integrated learners know where they want to go, enjoy being responsible for their own learning, and want freedom (within some structure) to accomplish specific tasks and assignments without much outside guidance.

Integrated learners are self-directed and demand quality from others as well as themselves. They want their work to be good and well integrated with overall objectives. Because integrated learners know what they want to learn and have used processes to learn on their own, trainers do not need to tell them precisely how to undertake specific learning tasks.

Risk-Taking Learners

Risk-taking learners thrive on learning new skills and information. They like to deviate from traditional course content and techniques and change their routines and schedules. Risk-taking learners are willing to work hard to meet goals, particularly if they will benefit from learning new concepts. They will stray from course guidelines happily if straying presents an opportunity to gain new knowledge.

Trainers can use the emerging design for risk-taking learners. Trainers need not be concerned if they have sketchy materials because risk-taking learners will welcome the opportunity for interactive exercises.

Adult Learning Principles

Adult learning principles provide a framework for development that helps ensure that participants learn. The acronym LEARN is useful in remembering some of these aspects of adult learning.

- **Learner directed:** If adults understand why they need the information you give them, the lesson will be easier for them to learn.
- **Experiential:** Adults in a learning environment gain more from experiencing the concepts being taught than they do from just a lecture or presentation. They want active involvement and relevance to their job and organization. This involves practicing and applying the concepts.
- **Able to be evaluated:** When teaching a concept, define it. Specify as clearly as possible the result you want from the learners. Identify what change in knowledge, skill, or attitude will take place.
- **Residual:** Adults learn more effectively if they build on known information, facts, or experiences rather than from independent, arbitrary facts. Base the

information provided on their experience and knowledge, and lead them into more depth of knowledge.

▼ **Numerous instructional methods:** Some people learn better from verbal instructions, some from written instructions, and some from examples. Others are visually oriented; and still others learn by trial and error. To reach a wider audience, incorporate various instructional methods in the program because different methods provide valuable reinforcement and make learning more interesting.

Adults vary greatly in the following areas:

▼ knowledge about their work
▼ pride in their work
▼ motivation to perform better
▼ maturity
▼ security
▼ learning styles
▼ expectations about the trainer
▼ expectations about what the training will do for them.

The last may be the most important of these areas. For training to be effective, trainees must believe that it is designed to be beneficial for them and not simply to increase their employer's productivity or to fulfill their manager's obligations to provide training programs.

Adult learners may enter their first training with expectations similar to those they had when they were in school. Much more is expected of adult learners; well-designed training involves trainees actively in the learning process. Adult learning styles vary. Training experts have found the following general approaches useful when designing training for the learner:

▼ Focus on real-world problems.
▼ Emphasize how trainees can apply what they are learning.
▼ Relate the learning to the trainees' goals.
▼ Relate the materials and new knowledge presented to the trainees' experience.
▼ Allow trainees to debate and challenge ideas.
▼ Listen to and respect trainees' opinions.

You must be familiar with the following 10 learning principles to design and develop appropriate trainings: (1) part or whole learning, (2) spaced learning, (3) active learning, (4) feedback, (5) overlearning, (6) reinforcement, (7) primacy and recency, (8) meaningful material, (9) multiple-sense learning, and (10) transfer of learning.

Part or Whole Learning

Part learning is more common than whole learning because trainees prefer dealing with a series of separate assignments. In part learning, the skill or knowledge is divided into parts. In whole learning, the skill or knowledge is looked at as a large, unified block of material. When dividing the material into parts, the trainer should use two guidelines:

▼ The parts should not be too large. Although it's familiar to you, the material will be new to the trainees. Therefore, review the skill or knowledge from the trainees' perspective, and then organize it into segments for training.

▼ The parts should follow a logical sequence. Put the material in an appropriate sequence so the trainees can relate each part to the next. A logical flow will enhance learners' ability to recall the skill or information. Proceed from the known to the unknown, moving from one part to the next after you know by the trainees' behaviors that they have understood and accepted the information. (Caution: Do not oversimplify. After separating the material into parts and developing a logical sequence, check to make sure the parts are not so small as to be boring.)

Consider teaching someone to ride a bicycle. This training should be divided into three parts: balancing, steering, and pedaling. Learning each part independently would be difficult because steering depends on balancing and on how hard the pedals are pushed, and balancing depends on steering and pedaling. Teaching someone to ride a bicycle requires whole learning. Whole learning is fairly uncommon; most training models are based on part learning.

Spaced Learning

Spaced learning usually is superior to crammed learning if trainees are to retain the material long-term. Spaced learning has its basis in what we know about incubation. The brain needs time to assimilate a particular group of facts before it can accept the next group of facts. Spaced learning creates opportunities for regular review and revision, which slows down the rate at which trainees forget material.

Active Learning

Involving trainees actively in the training rather than having them listen passively encourages trainees to become self-motivated. Active learning is more effective than passive learning and is often described as learning by doing. Provide trainees plenty of opportunity to practice using the skills and information they are learning.

Feedback

The feedback principle of learning has two aspects:

- Trainees need constructive feedback on their progress.
- Trainers need feedback on their own performance.

Feedback to trainees can vary in complexity from explaining why an answer is correct or incorrect to commenting on trainees' performance or discussing results of a test. Regardless of the complexity of the feedback, the best feedback is the one given the earliest. The more immediate the feedback, the greater its value, especially for preventing loss of self-confidence and, thus, loss of motivation.

Feedback to trainers answers the following questions:

- Are trainees receiving and understanding the information? (Test trainees for this.)
- Do trainees have doubts or questions? (Ask them.)
- Are all trainees paying attention? (Observe them.)
- Is the session boring? (Observe them.)
- Would trainees benefit by using more techniques during this session? (Ask them.)

Two-way communication is critical to feedback's effectiveness.

Overlearning

Overlearning means learning until trainees have near-perfect recall, and then learning the material just a bit more, perhaps through practice. Overlearning decreases the rate of forgetting. In other words, forgetting is significantly reduced by frequency recall or use of the material. Two important facts will help you:

- Trainers' repetition does not maximize retention.
- Trainees' active involvement maximizes retention.

Reinforcement

Reinforcement is one way to improve learning because learning that is rewarded is much more likely to be retained. A simple, "Yes, that's right," can mean a great deal to trainees and can enhance their retention considerably. Positive reinforcement confirms the value of responding and participating and encourages active learning, whereas negative reinforcement simply tells trainees that their responses were wrong without providing guidelines about which responses would have been correct. Negative reinforcement often discourages trainees from further investigation.

Primacy and Recency

When they are presented with a sequence of information, trainees tend to remember what they heard first and what they heard last, but they often forget what they heard in the middle. To guard against this, emphasize and reinforce facts that are in the middle, or present critical information at the beginning or end of the session.

Meaningful Material

Unconsciously, trainees ask these questions when presented with new information:

  ▼ Is this information valid relative to my experiences?
  ▼ Will this information be useful in the immediate future?

The first question emphasizes the notion of moving from the known to the unknown as well as the fact that people tend to remember material that relates to what they already know. In designing the training session, make sure to assess trainees' current levels of knowledge.

The second question emphasizes the fact that trainees want to know that what they are about to learn will be useful to them in the near future. Meaningful material links the past and the future and promotes two beneficial effects: security (when trainees move from the known to the unknown) and motivation (information will be useful in the near future).

Multiple-Sense Learning

Research suggests that of the information people absorb, they will obtain approximately 80 percent through sight, 11 percent through hearing, and 9 percent through all other senses combined. Therefore, to absorb as much as possible, trainers should design sessions to use two or more of the senses. Sight and hearing are straightforward, but designing sessions to use other senses, such as touch, might be just as crucial to successful learning. For most learning, however, sight provides the most information, so trainers should emphasize visual aids when designing their sessions. (For more on visual aids, see chapter 10.)

Transfer of Learning

The amount of learning that trainees transfer from the training room to the workplace depends mainly on these variables:

  ▼ the degree of similarity between what they learned in the training session (including how it was presented) and what occurs in the workplace (Can trainees apply their new knowledge and skills directly to the job without modifying them?)

▼ the degree to which trainees can integrate the skills and knowledge gained in the training session into their work environment (Does the system at work or the supervisor allow or encourage using the new skills?).

Consider these variables as you plan your training program. Make 3x5 inch cards that define the lesson and the objective. These cards are tools that trainees can take with them to use as references back on the job. Develop a checklist of all the learning outcomes for the training. Have learners check off outcomes as they perform them when they are on the job. Either provide learners with journals to use to record their progress after the training or check with each learner approximately one month after the training to get feedback on the training transfer.

Instructional Elements

When designing the training session, trainers should address the following 10 instructional elements: expectations, measurement, capacity, prerequisites, attitudes and motivation, instruction instructional resources, feedback, motivational climate, and performance support.

Expectations

Clarifying expectations, learning objectives, or learning goals is key to designing the training session. From the beginning, trainees must understand the desired outcome of the training and the relationship between that outcome and their jobs. It is not sufficient to define the learning objectives as part of your introduction. Throughout the session you must reiterate the objectives that you have integrated into the session design. By adhering to the following guidelines in your consideration of expectations, you will be well on your way to designing successful training sessions:

▼ Write clearly and directly.
▼ Explain the reason for the training.
▼ Relate the training to work performance.
▼ Clarify management's role.
▼ Negotiate and discuss with trainees to gain their ownership of the training.
▼ Review regularly, and revise, if necessary.

Measurement

Expectations are more likely to be met fully if the training design incorporates the means by which the trainer, trainees, and management can measure progress toward accomplishing them. Incorporate the following elements into the design:

▼ measurable training objectives
▼ measurable performance requirements aligned with training requirements

▼ methods that do not threaten trainees

▼ methods that allow for self- or peer measurement.

Capacity

Successful training can occur only if trainees have the capacities to succeed. Therefore, trainers should

▼ identify capacity requirements for training and job performance

▼ screen prospective trainees for physical, intellectual, or emotional capacity prior to their selection as part of the group

▼ provide opportunities for remedial training whenever possible and appropriate for trainees who do not meet certain capacity requirements.

Prerequisites

After taking the steps to ensure that trainees have the capacity to do the job for which the training is being designed, you may find that some trainees lack certain skills and the requisite knowledge base. Failure to address these gaps when designing the session would not be fair either to the trainees with the deficits or to those with the requisite skills and knowledge base.

▼ Specify clearly and in advance the prerequisites for the training.

▼ Study the trainees' characteristics.

▼ Administer pretests when possible and appropriate.

▼ Ask questions randomly to determine the trainees' general level of preparation.

▼ Design the training to meet the group's knowledge level (aim at the middle, see chapter 10).

▼ Prepare alternative routes through the course of instruction on the basis of the group's preparation level.

Attitudes and Motivation

Trainees must have positive attitudes and be motivated to benefit from training. As a trainer, you can increase the likelihood that trainees will have positive attitudes in the following ways:

▼ Do what you can to ensure that trainees are informed well in advance about the forthcoming training session.

▼ Exclude threatening or competitive issues from your materials and content.

▼ Include input from the trainees and union leadership (if relevant) in the design.

▼ Relate training to job requirements.

- Encourage prospective trainees to volunteer to attend.
- Build adequate amenities, such as beverages, lunch, and food, for breaks into the program. (You don't have to provide amenities equal to those from a luxury spa, but trainees should not feel as if they are in boot camp.)

Instruction

Although the design of instructional materials is extremely important to successful training, materials cannot substitute for high-quality instruction. By adhering to the following guidelines, trainers can ensure that their instruction will be top notch:

- Involve the entire trainee population in icebreakers and a discussion of their expectations.
- Demonstrate the skills or the learning that is to be trained.
- Provide brief and to-the-point content.
- Encourage feedback at every step.
- Build in several opportunities for trainees to practice.
- Pace the training to the trainees' level.
- Allow significant time for questions and answers.

Instructional Resources

Remember that you are training people to perform in their regular work settings. The training you provide must, therefore, be easy for them to transfer from your session and replicate at their jobs. Trainees who lack appropriate resources when they return to their work settings will not be able to replicate what they have learned. Understanding that this may be the case, you need to know what resources trainees will have available to them before you design the training session. Be sure to do the following:

- Request an inventory of resources.
- Conduct an inventory of resources.
- Incorporate the resources into the training design.
- Identify as many as possible of the following instructional resources:
  — follow-up information
  — reference materials
  — allocated time to practice
  — individuals assigned to help trainees apply what they learned
  — support materials, such as training videos.

Feedback

Feedback is critical to the success of any type of training. Trainees need to receive clear, appropriate, and timely information about their performance both in the training session and on the job. Feedback systems should be designed to provide trainees with performance-based information that specifically takes into account what they have learned in training, especially during the first several weeks following the training session. Three types of feedback are especially important:

▼ trainer's feedback, in staff and team meetings
▼ supervisor's positive feedback
▼ peer trainees' corrective feedback, provided it is given with sensitivity.

Remind all those involved that feedback must be based on specific information that the person receiving the feedback understands and on performance that the person can apply.

Motivational Climate

Positive attitudes and motivation are critical to effective training and performance. To a large extent, motivational climate determines whether attitudes are positive or negative and the direction and strength of motivation. Determine if any factors are adversely affecting learning performance and, if they are, correct the problems by

▼ removing constraints and barriers to learning and performance
▼ ensuring that positive consequences follow positive performance
▼ ensuring that negative consequences do not follow positive performance
▼ developing a supportive, trusting environment for learning and performance
▼ providing opportunities for participation
▼ increasing follow-through on employees' suggestions.

Performance Support

Frequently the link between training and on-the-job performance is tenuous or neglected. To support performance once trainees have returned to work, suggest to management the following:

▼ Hold follow-up meetings that include trainees.
▼ Provide trainees with adequate opportunities to use their new skills and knowledge.
▼ Reinforce what trainees learned.
▼ Empower trainees to explore new areas.
▼ Allow trainees to fail at new endeavors without penalizing them.
▼ Integrate supervisors into the training process.

Training Designs

Two general types of design, which may be viewed on a continuum, are available. At one end is a totally preplanned design, and at the other is an emerging design.

In a preplanned design, the trainer decides everything in advance for each session. Of course, be open to the reality that you may need to alter, rearrange, add, or drop your plans. However, understand that to design successful training programs, you must adhere to the goals, techniques, and evaluation criteria that you established in advance. The new or relatively inexperienced trainer should use a preplanned design.

Below are some guidelines for a preplanned design:

▼ Avoid overplanning, especially minute-by-minute outlines.
▼ Allow for flexibility.
▼ Prepare for some resistance to change if feedback during the training indicates the need to make changes.

In an emerging design, little is decided in advance. By designing at the moment, the trainer maximizes the effect of the trainees' experiences and interactions on the training activity. Sometimes an emerging design will have a plan only for the opening session, with the remainder of the plan emerging as the training proceeds. An emerging design requires minimal preplanning and maximum trainer skills.

Following are some guidelines for emerging designs:

▼ Advertise the training activity accurately so that trainees will know that a flexible design will be used.
▼ Adhere to the design.
▼ Stop occasionally during the training to ask yourself, "Is this producing learning in accordance with our goals?"

Whatever design you use, remember that adult learners absorb material best when it is given during presentations, demonstrations, readings, dramas, discussions, case studies, visual aids, role plays, games, and participant-directed inquiries.

Trainer Styles

Adult learners bring rich life experiences to your training. Members of this group

▼ make their own decisions about which aspects of the training are important
▼ validate the information presented based on their specific beliefs and experiences
▼ have a lot of experience and fixed viewpoints
▼ bring significant knowledge to the training
▼ expect what they learn to be useful immediately.

During their formal education process, many adult learners found that they could best learn and use the information from a certain kind of instructor. There are three trainer styles: authoritarian, laissez-faire, and democratic. Each style affects the learning process.

At one extreme is the authoritarian style, which tends to dominate the learning process by having the information flow in a one-way process from the trainer to the learner. This style leaves little room for learners to interact with the trainer. In training, the authoritarian style of communication limits learning.

At the other extreme is the laissez-faire style. It may lead the learners to feel that there is too little direction and that the learning experience is disorganized and not well planned. The trainer might establish the focus of the conversation, for example, and then turn the dialogue over to the trainees for them to manage the direction, content, and flow of the exchange. Using the laissez-faire style of communication in training may confuse learning.

The democratic style offers a more balanced approach. The trainer establishes an in-session dialogue with the trainees. Both the trainer and trainees have equal responsibility to promote the topic. This approach allows for the interplay of personalities among the trainer and the learners. With the democratic style of communication in the training, the instructional foundation is solid and learning is collaborative.

Summary

Learning objectives are the most important element in the design and development process. The learning objectives define the topic, the content, and, to some degree, the learning and teaching processes. Remember to always have the three essential components in every objective:

▼ the performance statement, the action or behavior the learner must exhibit after the training event

▼ the condition, the tools, equipment, or document necessary to be used in the learning process

▼ the criteria, the level of standard that the learner's performance must meet.

Organize and design the content you are to teach with the five learner styles in mind. The five styles are

▼ the confident learner
▼ the affective learner
▼ the transitional learner
▼ the integrated learner
▼ the risk-taking learner.

The acronym LEARN, as explained earlier, defines the essential design guidelines involving adult learning:

▼ Learner directed
▼ Experiential
▼ Able to be evaluated
▼ Residual
▼ Numerous instructional methods.

The steps define the adult learning principles that provide the framework for organizing the learning process. These principles ensure that your design will be structured so that adult learners can participate in the learning process and not feel anxious about events that will happen during the learning process.

In addition, establish and design your training design format using the 10 following instructional elements.

1. Clarify expectations.
2. Develop an outcome measurement mechanism.
3. Cluster content around the learners' capacity.
4. Provide prerequisites when you present new information.
5. Take steps to ensure that trainees had positive attitudes.
6. Follow guidelines to high-quality instruction.
7. Identify instructional resources for further mastery beyond the training.
8. Provide feedback.
9. Assess motivational climate.
10. Integrate adult learning principles in your design and delivery strategies.

Check-Up Exercise

1. What are the three essential components of an objective?
2. What are the five learning styles?
3. The acronym LEARN defines the essential design guidelines involving adult learning. What does it stand for?
4. Describe the 10 elements that you need to consider for your training design format.

Development

eveloping training is the process of creating, testing, and producing usable instructional materials for your training event. Now that you have identified your training topic, and created your learning objectives and test items, you are ready to develop the course works.

The term *course works* is used to define those materials that you are going to develop to use in your training. Course works include participant workbooks, instructor guide, handouts, presentation slides, wall charts, and various instructional materials, such as games, checklists, policies, or regulations.

Throughout the developing process, you should always include your training team members to assist you in making decisions about the course curriculum, course training material, and instructional materials. If you have not already done so, organize a training team. This team should include those who are knowledgeable in the content area, instructional design, and evaluation. The team's role should be to continually review the major training materials that are developed in this step. In addition, call on

▼▼▼

Determine if the training you are to provide is focusing on education (theory) or training (skill training). If the answer is education, then the most important question to answer before finalizing the training material is, "What has been the previous success or failure of the learners in the educational setting?" If the answer is training, then look at the skill set or competencies that must be acquired or mastered.

▲▲▲

the team to review the revisions and use the pilot training test to check the program materials prior to the actual delivery of the training.

Training should be developed and delivered in partnership with line managers to establish a clear link between what happens in training and what happens on the job. Training should be all about individuals becoming effective in their roles and responsibilities. By equipping individuals with a clear definition of the requirements of the job and the required skill set to perform the job, employees will be motivated and open to change.

Develop the Curriculum

Now that you have identified your audience needs and established your learning objectives and test items, you are ready to organize your topic and subtopics. The training contains topic courses. Each course consists of learning modules, and each module consists of a number of lessons, depending on the complexity of your topic.

The term *curriculum* means "course of study." Organizing the instructional content for your training program begins with reviewing the research and structuring the topics into logical units of related content. The content is further organized into specific learning modules. The modules are developed by structuring the subtopics into smaller units of content known as lessons.

Once you have developed the modules and lessons, start writing your lesson plans for each of the lessons in your modules—it's a little like developing a macro scheme that lists all the course content you want to teach, and then developing the content on a micro level. Now that you have identified your modules and your lesson using your lesson plan, you are ready to develop your course works.

Once the content units are organized, select the instructional strategy that best meets the training objective and learner outcomes. All elements of the training program are determined during the development step. These elements include the specific course manuals, all integrated into the training plan, designed to achieve the training objectives.

The instructional specifications serve as a blueprint for program development because they determine what content to include, when to include it, and why. They also serve as the foundation for evaluation activities.

Course design is linked to course development through a series of documents. From these documents, you create your initial blueprint. The blueprint should list the course objectives. Supportive information about the course content should then be linked to each objective. You also may want to identify which objectives are to be met in the training presentation and which apply to the workplace.

Define the Content

Training and content experts work together to select the instructional content. They systematically define the critical content modules and show how the instructional strategies will introduce content. In addition, they determine appropriate learning techniques, develop opportunities for practice, and select appropriate media. Remember, all the media should have a definite purpose; you choose them to amplify learning, not to entertain a bored audience.

The instructional specifications include

▼ module name

▼ introduction (content summary, utility, importance)

▼ sequence of topics and activities (flow, transitions, links).

For each objective, there should be documentation elaborating the following:

▼ special teaching points

▼ instructional methods

▼ media requirements

▼ testing requirements.

Develop Content Sequence

You should develop the training sequence in a logical order. Frequently, more than one logical order may be appropriate. You must choose the sequencing method most suited to the learning tasks and demographics of the group.

The usual sequences are step by step, simple to complex, or overview to detailed learning. Step by step is a good choice if a task is always done in a certain order. Simple to complex is better when it's appropriate to have learners develop simple skills first, and then build on them to learn more complex skills. When it's appropriate for learners to know how an entire process works before they learn its separate tasks, they should get an overview before detailed learning.

At this point, select the overall training strategies. Details can be worked out when specific materials are chosen. For now, make general decisions about the training method and the training media. Ask yourself, "Will the course include on-the-job training, classroom instruction, lab or workshop instruction, or self-instruction?" "Will the course use textbooks, workbooks, computers, interactive CD-ROMs, audiotapes, or videotapes?"

The strategies you select must match the stated objectives of the training. For example, the strategies for a course to help trainees master computer skills should not rely heavily on pencil-and-paper activities. Participants would need opportunities for hands-on computer practice to pass a job-related evaluation at the course's end.

Create Test Items

The second step in developing instructional strategies is to design test items to be used during the training to check on the progress of learning. Well-written objectives call for learners to demonstrate observable, measurable actions. Objectives shouldn't include verbs like *understand* or *know* because they describe a learner's internal state, which cannot be observed.

Ask yourself if the objective is really a test of the learner's ability to describe work or of the person's ability to do work. By looking at objectives in terms of how they will be tested, you may want to identify subordinate skills and knowledge that were overlooked during the task analysis. Your main task is to identify and correct poor objectives before training materials are developed to support them.

The objective should be a well-defined outcome. Once the objective is defined, it serves as the master blueprint for course and module development as well as supporting instructional and participant materials. However, this degree of detail is often lacking in objectives. Moreover, objectives may not be an effective set of documents to communicate outcomes to your client, but the end-of-course criterion test would be.

The criterion test is another part of the blueprint that will help you develop the training. If the training is long enough to warrant intermediate mastery tests, you should specify the behaviors to be measured at each checkpoint, along with any suggestions on the format of the test. You should place whatever format you select for the blueprint in a reference binder for subsequent use by the following people:

- the course developer and suppliers in specialized media
- the instructor to get an overview of the content of the course
- the training department staff to counsel employees on which course to take
- the managers to determine if a course contains specific material for themselves or their staff.

Write the Lesson Plan

Once you've completed your course and module design, your next step is to develop a lesson plan. The set of detailed notes that you write will guide you through the material development and delivery processes. The elements of a lesson should include the following:

- session title
- learning objectives
- timing
- key learning points

- brief content synopsis
- presentation methodology
- definition of terms
- key questions to ask
- resource requirements
- learner activities
- topic transitions
- review checks
- learner issues.

The format of the suggested lesson plan includes five columns: timing, content, training techniques, trainee activity, and training aids. Following is a description of each item:

- **Timing.** List the time you will spend on each topic and subtopic of each session. A typical training day is six hours, and you have 55 minutes in an hour for training. You should allot 10 percent of the time to introduce or make a transition to the topic, and devote 70 percent of the time to content delivery, which might include preparing the learner to learn (stating the objective), presenting the material, and practicing the material with an exercise and feedback. The final 20 percent of the time should be devoted to summary, conclusion, and transition to the next lesson or module.

- **Content.** List the topic and subtopics that you will cover during each session. Do not combine sessions. Develop and deliver each session topic independently, using transitional statements to bridge from one topic or subtopic to another. In the session plan, indicate introductions, breaks, and sequences in one session. Don't have run-on sessions without using transition statements. Run-on sessions are those that continue after a lunch or other break or even from one day to the next. Deliver your content in complete and inclusive parts. Illogical breaks that occur because trainers did not scope the content appropriately leave the trainer in an awkward situation and the learning incomplete.

- **Training techniques.** Explain in basic terms whether the session is to be a lecture, show and tell, or participant discovery.

- **Trainee activity.** List the types of things that the learner will be doing during the session (listening, looking, practicing). By documenting this information, you'll have the opportunity to build a variety of activities into your training course in advance.

▼ **Training aids.** List the instructional aids and strategies or peripherals that you'll use and the order in which you'll use them.

Too much information at one time creates confusion. *Chunking* is the term for breaking down concepts into meaningful parts. Give a learner a maximum of three large pieces of information. In a module, if you have three major components to the topic, deliver them within an hour. Once you deliver the three large chunks within an hour, it's time to summarize and break.

Cluster the topical information that you have researched in organized sections, such as introduction, body, and activities. Next, use the technique of grading the content to target the correct amount of information to deliver. Figure 9-1 shows a simple way of grading the material you'll deliver.

The must-know information is the enabling knowledge that the learner needs to know to perform the task or job. The need-to-know information may be needed for the learner to gain a clear understanding of the essential information presented during the session. The nice-to-know information encompasses items that are not necessary to know and might illustrate the points covered in the session.

It's reasonable for you to assume that if you develop your instruction at the bull's-eye, the must-know area, a certain amount of time also would be spent in the need-to-know area as a review. If time permits, let the learners look at the nice-to-know area, but the time would probably be better spent reviewing the need-to-know and must-know areas. You must deliver too little well, rather than too much badly.

A lesson plan allows you to determine in advance if the delivery sequence is correct, the content is relevant to the topic and the learner, and your instructional strategies are appropriate. The lesson plan also acts as a resource checklist. It allows you to prepare for any information or material that may be required for the lesson, such as handouts, overheads, videotapes, flipcharts, and wall charts. The essential elements in the lesson plan are timing, learning objectives, brief summaries of each topic point, learner and trainer activities, and needed materials. The structure of the session plan should be a format that you feel comfortable using.

▼▼▼

As you write your plan, ask yourself two questions:

- "What is the purpose of this training presentation?"
- "What do learners need to know about the topic?"

▲▲▲

Figure 9-1. Technique to grade content.

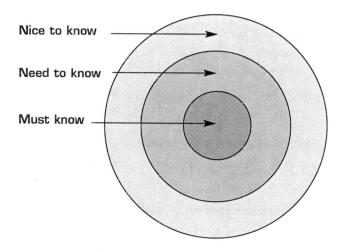

Source: G. McArdle, *Delivering Effective Training Sessions* (Menlo Park, CA: Crisp Publications, 1993).

Select Instructional Strategies

The choice of an appropriate instructional strategy for a particular audience is, at best, a guess if you have not been able to conduct a formal audience needs analysis. One way to avoid mismatching an instructional strategy with a particular audience is to be sensitive to an organization's demographics and preferences.

Technology choice should be suitable for the audience, the content, the organizational environment, and, most of all, the proposed learning objective. These preferences provide you with

▽ a design template to assist in developing the content of your course material
▽ a checklist for making decisions about learning activities.

▼▼▼

Do not make your lesson plan too elaborate or complicated. The lesson plan is a road map, your course map, to help you organize your course, from the beginning through the end. By referring to it as you present your program, you may find it assists your delivery as well.

▲▲▲

The intent of any training should be to promote behavior change through learning. Instruction promotes learning through a set of events developed to initiate, activate, and support learning. Use instructional strategies to

▼ motivate learners
▼ help learners prepare for learning
▼ enable learners to apply and practice learning
▼ assist learners to retain and transfer what they have learned.

Instructional strategies, sometimes called presentation strategies, are the mechanisms through which instruction is presented. The most common strategies are the following:

▼ **Lecture**. The course instructor presents the content of the course. Communication is primarily one way, from the instructor to the learner.
▼ **Role play**. Participants act out situations and assume roles that they play spontaneously to emphasize concepts presented.
▼ **Group discussion**. Class members discuss a given topic. Ideas are accepted from all participants.
▼ **Self-discovery**. Learners discover the content of the course on their own by using a variety of techniques, such as research and guided exercises.
▼ **Self-paced/programmed instruction**. Learners read or perform course-related activities, progressing through the program at their own pace.
▼ **Case study**. Learners analyze situations and draw conclusions or recommend solutions on the basis of the content presented in the course.
▼ **Competitive game**. Learners compete against one another in teams or as individuals in a fun-based activity where one team or individual is the winner.
▼ **Cooperative game**. Learners work together in teams or as individuals in a fun-based activity to reach a common goal in which all teams or individuals win.
▼ **Movie/video**. Content comes primarily from movies or videotapes.
▼ **Individual project**. Learners work individually to apply the concepts presented in the course.
▼ **Group project**. Learners work in teams to apply the concepts presented in the course.
▼ **Simulation**. Learners participate in a reality-based, interactive activity that imitates a more complex simulation.

Instructional Strategy

The appropriate strategy to use for a presentation depends on a variety of factors:

- ▼ type of learning (verbal information, intellectual skills, cognitive strategy, attitude, motor skills)
- ▼ audience
- ▼ demographics or profile (age, gender, level of education)
- ▼ learning styles (kinesthetic-tactile, visual, auditory)
- ▼ number of learners (individual, small groups, large groups)
- ▼ media (selected by appropriateness, number of learners, financial considerations)
- ▼ budget (funds available for development as well as presentation)
- ▼ physical site (centralized, decentralized, specialized)
- ▼ instructor's skills and training style.

Each factor, in combination with the others, influences the choice of a strategy for presenting, reinforcing, and assessing the retention of the material. A model depicting the relationship among these factors is shown in figure 9-2.

Learner Preferences

As you develop your training, assume that the audience is more likely to participate when the material is presented in a relaxed, informal learning environment that is conducive to the trainees' and the trainer's interactions. A learning environment that

Figure 9-2. Factors influencing instructional strategy.

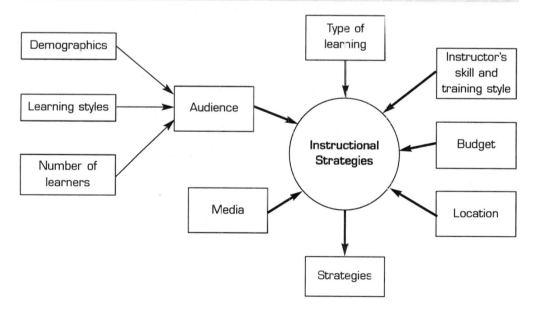

is relaxed but structured—with agenda, objectives, and established timeframes and tasks—is one in which participants will participate and, therefore, is one in which the learning will be successful. There is a relationship between the target audience's demographics and their preferences for particular instructional strategies. A conducive learning environment leads to

- increased attention and motivation
- increased mastery
- more successful transfer of what's been learned back to the learner's own environment
- enhanced retention and recall.

By understanding the trainees' profiles and demographics, you are more likely to be sensitive to the instructional strategies the trainees prefer. In most cases, during your analysis and design process, you have only basic information about the target audience:

- age (usually a range)
- gender
- occupation (current as well as previous on occasion)
- ethnicity (known only occasionally because of Equal Employment Opportunity Commission considerations)
- years of work experience (usually a range).

The demographics alone do not reveal a learner's preference, although this information is a good starting place. Group discussions tend to be one of the training methods people like most, followed by case studies, games, and role playing. Lectures and telecommunication methods such as video lectures are two of the methods people like least. Videotapes, intrapersonal and interpersonal training, and self-instruction and computer-based instruction fall in the middle. By discovering which instructional strategies different groups prefer, you are better able to develop and deliver training that specific audiences like and consider motivating.

In the 1970s, David McClelland, a psychologist, used the works of Carl Jung to identify predominant learning styles (Blanchard & Thacker, 2003). McClelland asserted that there are three main learning style preferences:

- Hepatic learners, also called kinesthetic-tactile learners, learn best when they are involved, moving, experiencing, and experimenting.
- Visual learners learn best when they see pictures of what they are studying. A small percentage are print-oriented and learn best by reading.
- Auditory learners learn best through sound, such as music and talk.

Learner Motivations

Responding to adult learners' preferences for one instructional strategy over another can help you improve trainees' motivation to learn. Success, volition, value, and enjoyment create motivated learners. When you develop your material, you can enhance motivation by relating learning to age-specific adult interests and using relevant topics to set the stage regardless of the specific instructional design. One way to reach trainees of different stages during a session is to use a variety of examples. An example about being a parent, for example, would not be helpful to trainees who had no children.

Obtain Instructional Resources

Support requirements include materials, equipment, and administrative support. They include computers, flipcharts, and other logistical support you need to design, develop, implement, and evaluate the training. It is critical to identify support requirements to ensure that necessary support resources will be available when you need them.

Establish Design Requirements

When you have the objectives and the media requirements, you can estimate the support resources you'll need and the number of days the training program should last.

Table 9-1 identifies some of the typical items necessary for running a training program. Itemized lists like this can help trainers make sure that they've arranged all the support personnel and materials they need for their programs.

Develop a Course Map

Adult learners respond best to small, organized units of learning, so organize the course content into modules. A lesson is the smallest unit of learning and provides content and practice on the basis of predefined learning objectives. Each lesson relates to a specific task in the task analysis, so that at the end of the training, learners should be able to perform the task.

Each learning module contains the following:

▼ objectives
▼ knowledge content to enable the learners to complete the task
▼ task content
▼ practice activities to help reach the objectives
▼ an assessment mechanism to determine if the objectives were achieved.

Table 9-1. Support requirements checklist.

Items	Date Required:	Date Ordered:	Cost:
Travel and lodging costs			
Travel and lodging arrangements			
Consultant fees			
Graphics			
Reproduction (e.g., notebooks, job aids)			
Documentation production schedule			
Materials (e.g., tabs, binders)			
Compile binders			
Gifts, prizes, mementos			
Temporary personnel			
Facility availability			
Equipment availability			
Evaluation forms			
Media arrangements			
Instructor scheduling			
Instructor training			
Software costs			
Software reproduction			
Software distribution			
Legal review			

Source: Author, 1995.

The module design serves as a major section of your course blueprint for developing the content and instructional strategies. To create a module, consider the following elements in each module you design:

- State the objective.
- Identify content topics.
- Identify trainer and learner activities that will result in mastery of the objective, including methods and media used by trainer and learner.

Having completed the task analysis, written the objectives, and designed the test items, you now have a good idea of what is going to be included in the training program. The next step is to outline the information and develop a course map, which identifies all the steps that lead to the completion of the course. Some people develop the course map as soon as they have completed the job and task analysis, whereas others wait until they have begun to develop the course materials and instructional strategies. Either way, it is critical to keep your audience and the purpose of the course in mind as you develop it.

The course map lists in hierarchical order the modules within units, as figure 9-3 shows. Some trainers describe the hierarchy as modules within chapters or as units within lessons within modules. The terminology is not important.

This map is accompanied by media selections and support requirements. (Note: The analogous map for computer-based training may be a skeleton storyboard, which shows frame by frame what will appear in the computer training.)

You should think about these influences on your course as you design the course map and ensure that the design is consistent with them:

▾ course objectives
▾ class size
▾ training site
▾ pre- and post-coursework
▾ course materials
▾ delivery strategy and instructor needs
▾ multilevel audience experience
▾ course relationship to job conditions
▾ learner motivation and accountability.

Let's consider a course in problem analysis. You have created your objectives, your test items, and your topic content. You are now ready to develop a course and module map. The first thing you do is list all of the elements that you consider necessary to teach. Next, you organize them in a logical framework, and then you develop subtopics. Here is an example of a course and module design for the topic problem analysis.

Chapter 1:   Problem Analysis
             Module 1: How to state the problem
             Module 2: How to define the standard
             Module 3: How to define the difference

Chapter 2:   Cause Identification
             Module 1: How to determine training deficiencies
             Module 2: How to determine other deficiencies

Figure 9-3. Example of a course map.

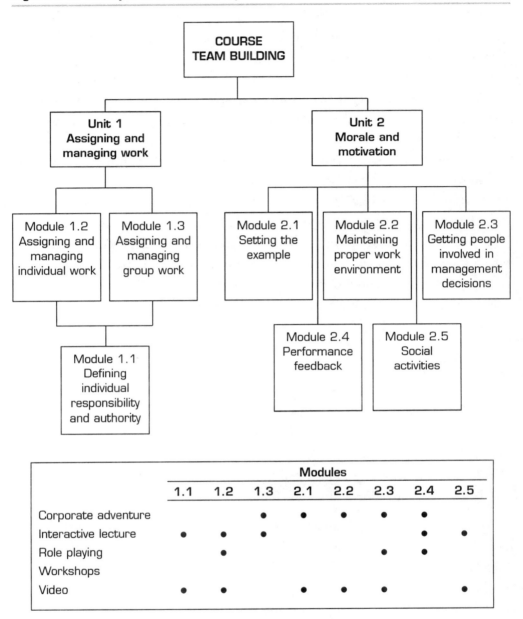

Chapter 3:   Data Collection
            Module 1: How to create data collection questions
            Module 2: How to use data collection sources
            Module 3: How to manage data collection

Chapter 4:   Idea Generation
            Module 1: How to use individual techniques
            Module 2: How to use group techniques

Chapter 5:   Solution Selection
            Module 1: How to evaluate ideas
            Module 2: How to select the best idea

Chapter 6:   Solution Implementation
            Module 1: How to manage resources
            Module 2: How to complete a time and action plan

Chapter 7:   Solution Evaluation
            Module 1: How to measure results
            Module 2: How to document results

Prepare a Design Report

The design report is a summary of the analysis and design completed to date. It serves as a preliminary communiqué to inform management of your progress and provides an opportunity for suggestions and feedback. It is a way to ensure that the training meets management's expectations because managers' support for your training objectives and course outcomes is critical to your success as well as the success of your program and the trainees.

The report serves to inform management of the proposed training; it provides a road map for the instructional designer to use in developing the training, and it provides the course instructor with background information with respect to how and why the training was developed.

A design report contains several narrative components:

▼ purpose of the course
▼ summary of the analysis
▼ scope of the course
▼ test item strategy
▼ course and module design
▼ delivery strategy
▼ level of evaluation to be tested.

▼ ▼ ▼

Consider the big picture when developing a course. Once you have identified the reasons for the course, your next step is to develop a course sequence. Here are some guidelines for sequencing the entire course:

- Focus on what happens on the job.
- Use the job analysis to establish the sequence of chapters.
- Arrange the course in sequence from general to specific, from simple to complex.
- Arrange the course in the most logical fashion for the learner when there is no job-related basis for sequencing.
- Use a model for performance as a guide for sequencing if available, such as a problem-solving or training design model.
- Use the same training advisory group to test the sequence as you did to validate other areas of your analysis and design process.

▲ ▲ ▲

Figure 9-4 is a sample design report for a problem-solving course for new managers.

Create Training Materials

During the development phase, you select, write, or otherwise obtain all training, documentation, and evaluation materials. These may include the following:

▼ training materials

▼ instructor guide (including lesson plans and a list of required supporting materials)

▼ trainees' guide or workbooks

▼ nonprint media (computer software, audiotapes and videotapes, equipment checklists)

▼ program evaluation materials

▼ procedures for training program evaluations

▼ course evaluation forms

▼ supervisors' forms for evaluation of course participants' post-training job performance

▼ training documentation

▼ class attendance forms and other records for training participants

▼ course documentation (written objectives, authorship and responsibility for course material, lists of instructors and facilitators, and their qualifications).

Figure 9-4. Sample design report.

Purpose of the Course

The course will introduce new managers to the established problem-solving strategies developed at our company. These problem-solving skills will be separated into sessions. The course will integrate current company issues into the program, rather than use issues discussed when the course was last held five years ago.

Summary of Analyses

Needs analysis and problem analysis: When the course was last given, these analyses led to the development of an internal problem-solving model for use during management sessions. That model was successful, but it needs updating.

Audience analysis: The company has 30 managers located in eight regions who need to learn the problem-solving model to participate more effectively in management meetings.

Job and task analysis: The problem-solving model already exists. We need to customize it to meet the new managers' needs and overcome questions about our new product line.

Scope of the Course

This course will use a seven-stage model of problem solving. The three-day course will be held at our corporate headquarters. All new managers will attend.

Task Learning Objective

Objective 1: Given the problem-solving model and one case-study scenario, resolve the customer question to the level of satisfaction of the instructor.

Objective 2: Given the product features guidelines and the problem-solving model, resolve the customer product complaint to the satisfaction of the customer within acceptable guidelines of the company policy.

Objective 3: List and define the steps in the problem-solving model by using all seven stages of the model in two case studies in the workshop. They will be assessed at the end of each chapter.

Training materials must support course objectives. Resources may be ready-made materials chosen for a specific course, customized materials designed for a specific course, materials taken from a previous course developed in-house, or materials purchased from vendors.

Off-the-shelf materials save development time. However, off-the-shelf material is generic, which means it can appeal to any audience. If you need the material to be customer focused, then you'll have to spend time and resources customizing it.

▼ ▼ ▼

The output of the development stage is a training program that is ready to be implemented. The development process consists of five phases, each one leading to the next. Following is a description of the phases.

- **Phase 1. Develop the following:**
  — training program content
  — graphics
  — media needs
  — lesson plans
  — instructor guides
  — evaluation needs
  — software needs.

- **Phase 2. Revise the following:**
  — training program content
  — graphics
  — media needs
  — lesson plans
  — instructor guides
  — evaluation needs
  — software needs.

- **Phase 3. Do the following:**
  — Conduct the test.
  — Revise the program on the basis of the test.
  — Schedule a second test, if needed.

- **Phase 4. Do the following:**
  — Pilot test a prototype program.
  — Evaluate the pilot test.
  — Identify the required revisions.
  — Revise the program as required (on the basis of the pilot test).
  — Schedule a second test, if needed.

- **Phase 5. Do the following:**
  — Finalize the training program content.
  — Produce the training program in final form.

▲ ▲ ▲

Make sure that you keep a library of all course materials that you use. It just might be that on occasion, you could use a predesigned module from an in-house customized course that would fit well with a new course you develop. That's OK. The material belongs to your company. It's better to have customized material than generic material in your training programs. You have more control of the content and the rationale for the designed components of the training.

Create Evaluation Materials

Evaluation forms should be easy to understand and require a minimum of time to complete. Plans should be made to ensure that the forms are completed and that they get collected, otherwise you'll get incomplete, and possibly invalid, information.

Once an evaluation is completed on a course, it's necessary to provide copies of the evaluations to the course developer, the course evaluator, and the course administrator. Each one of these key individuals evaluates the content of the evaluation remarks differently and acts on the content. For example, the developer looks for evaluative remarks concerning the topic treatment and the instructional events. This data will serve as the basis for course revisions.

Create Training Documentation Materials

Training records can be kept in paper files or on a computer. The course administrator can be responsible for maintaining the database.

Consider the Legal Implications

Since the 1960s, a number of federal laws were passed that require employers to provide equal opportunity in employment and career progression. All of these laws require employers to inform employees of their rights through posting the laws, related notices, and position openings. You should be familiar with the following laws that affect training and development.

Title VII, Civil Rights Act

Congress passed Title VII of the Civil Rights Act of 1964 to bring about equality in hiring, transferring, promoting, accessing training, and other employment-related decisions. Title VII also stipulated that there must be equal opportunity to participate in training programs. If employees have nondiscriminatory access to the same training, everyone will have the opportunity to be better qualified for advancement.

Age Discrimination in Employment Act

The Age Discrimination in Employment Act was enacted in 1967 to protect older workers. Generally, the ADEA protects workers over the age of 40 against employment discrimination on the basis of age. This protection includes giving qualified employees equal accessibility to training.

Americans With Disabilities Act

The Americans with Disabilities Act was modeled after the Vocational Rehabilitation Act of 1973 and the Rehabilitation Act of 1974. People with either mental or physical disabilities or limitations, or who are regarded as having such impairments, sometimes suffer from employment discrimination in that they are not considered for jobs that they are qualified for and are capable of doing. The ADA protects qualified individuals from unlawful discrimination in the workplace, including access to training and career development.

Defense Against Charges of Training Discrimination

It is not difficult to defend yourself against a charge of discrimination if you can show that your training programs are designed and delivered without bias. The following guidelines, from the Society for Human Resource Management (SHRM), apply to all of the employment laws discussed so far:

- ▼ Register affirmative action training and apprenticeship programs with the U.S. Department of Labor.
- ▼ Keep records of all employees who apply for enrollment in training programs and the details of how they were selected.
- ▼ Document all management decisions and actions that relate to the administration of training policies.
- ▼ Monitor each trainee's progress, provide evaluations, and ensure that counseling is available.
- ▼ Continue to evaluate results even after training is completed.

Labor Relations Statutes

Union activity between the 1930s and the mid-1950s provided the impetus for the development and passage of two acts that affect training and development: the National Labor Relations Act of 1935 and the Labor-Management Relations Act of 1947. The National Labor Relations Act, also referred to as the Wagner Act, prohibits discrimination against union members with respect to terms and conditions of employment, including apprenticeships and training programs. The National Labor Relations Board considers training to be a condition of employment and a mandatory subject for collective bargaining. The Labor-Management Relations Act, also known as the Taft-Hartley Act, prevents unions from discrimination for any reason except for payment of dues and assessments. The act also permits noncoercive employer free speech; this may affect trainers. For example, if your company president supports a particular political party, it could be assumed that you support that party.

In training, you should use no examples, case studies, or role plays that infringe upon a person's personal philosophy or belief system.

Copyright Statutes

Trainers try to use the very latest materials during training events. We must set an example that does not encourage others to use any material that requires prior permission for use unless that permission has been obtained.

The design and development of training programs likely require the use or incorporation of various sources of information. It is important to pay attention to copyright requirements. Copyright, explains Francine Ward, respected attorney and copyright and trademark law expert, "is a legal form of protection afforded to any original work of art or authorship that has been reduced to a tangible or physical form.... Copyright holders have the exclusive, but not the absolute, right to print, reprint, copy, or duplicate their work, which includes making photocopies, downloading music, and duplicating photographs." The Copyright Act of 1976 stipulates that copyright begins with the creation of the work in a fixed form from which it can be perceived or communicated. This statute also gives the author the right to distribute, display, perform, and prepare derivative works.

The exclusive rights of the author or proprietor are limited by the fair use of copyrighted works in certain circumstances. Whether a use is fair depends upon several factors, including

- purpose and character of the use
- nature of the copyrighted work
- amount of the work is being used and how substantial the portion is in relationship to the copyrighted work as a whole
- effect of the use upon the potential market for or value of the copyrighted work.

Fair use standards may apply to training materials. As a trainer, you can make a single copy of copyrighted materials for your own use. Check with the copyright holder before you make multiple copies of copyrighted materials. As SHRM points out, "if a trainer violates copyright statutes, the penalties can be severe and may include injunction, actual damages, defendant's lost profits, statutory damages, and attorney's fees."

For anonymous works and works made for hire (such as those prepared by trainers or other employees at the request of employers), the period of protection lasts for 75 years from the first year of publication or 100 years from the year of creation, whichever expires first. Employers, rather than the employees who did the writing, are considered authors of the work and the owners of the copyright. Registration of the copyright with the Copyright Office of the Library of Congress is not a condition of copyright protection; the law does, however, provide inducement to register works.

A work that has fallen into the public domain is available for use without permission from the copyright owner or payment to that person. A work is considered public domain if it meets one of the following characteristics:

- It was published prior to January 1, 1978, without notice of copyright.
- The period of copyright protection has expired.
- It was produced for the U.S. government by its officers or employees as part of their official duties.

Until recently, copyrights had little to do with the daily work of trainers. Intellectual property was easy to protect. However, with the advent of the Internet, it is easy for any computer user to copy, distribute, or publish almost anything. This technology threatens to make copyright and intellectual property safeguards obsolete. The Copyright Act blurs when it comes into contact with the Internet. However, messages or articles posted on a Usenet newsgroup or email are automatically copyrighted by the authors.

Prepare the Final Budget

The goal of training and professional development in most organizations is to make a positive, cost-effective change within the organization. Yet, the training department often appears as a departmental cost or organizational expense. Training provides significant return-on-investment and can be viewed as such rather than as a line-item expense in a budget.

Using traditional cost-accounting principles, you can show a return when you cost out your individual training programs. To do this, you must calculate the total cost of training. Next, indicate the savings or benefit to the organization. Finally, calculate the cost of training per employee. Here's the basic formula:

$$\text{Cost per trainee} = \frac{\text{Total cost of training}}{\text{Number of people trained}}$$

The information needed to justify the cost of training depends on a number of factors. Table 9-2 shows the categories of potential costs and benefits. Actual costs will vary depending on the training site and whether programs have been custom designed, purchased, or developed in-house.

You should include both direct and indirect costs in your overall training budget. Direct costs include regular operating costs, such as wages or salaries of participants and trainers as well as costs for travel, lodging, supplies, and materials that relate to a particular program. Indirect costs include secretarial and clerical help, use of telephone and audiovisual equipment, and costs associated with lower productivity when a worker is attending a training.

When you prepare a budget proposal, include estimated savings or increased profits that might result from implementing the training. Include supplemental details for each program such as the following: program length, space requirements, number of trainees per session, materials, equipment, instructors (both internal and external), and an estimate of the development and administrative costs.

Table 9-2. Potential training costs and benefits.

Potential Training Costs	Potential Benefits
• Trainer's salary	• Reduction in errors
• Trainee's salary or wage	• Increase in production
• Materials and supplies for training	• Reduction in turnover
• Consultant's services	• Reduction in supervision
• Living expenses for trainer and trainees	• Ability to advance
• Facilities	• Ability to perform wider range of jobs
• Transportation	• Attitude change
• Equipment	• Employee and organization alignment
• Lost production (opportunity cost)	• Facilitation of organizational change
• Development costs:	• Improved customer satisfaction
— Consultant's fees and expenses	• Increase in organizational
— Hours spent by staff professionals, clerical help, and line managers	competencies
• Support costs:	
— Postage	
— Data maintenance	
• Equipment costs:	
— Audiovisual	
— Computer	

Source: Reprinted with permission from the Society for Human Resource Management Certification Program, 1997.

Most trainers look at cost figures to measure the effect of training success. Cost figures are taken directly from the budget and can be found in three general categories:

- ▼ **Cost**: expense per unit of training delivered
- ▼ **Change**: gain in skill or knowledge by the learner
- ▼ **Impact**: results from the learner's use of new skills or knowledge.

No simple calculation can account for all possible training costs and benefits. However, the easiest calculation of return-on-investment (ROI) involves adding up all expenses (both direct and indirect) and dividing by the total number of people trained, as the following equation shows:

$$\frac{\text{Cost of training}}{\text{Cost of unwanted behavior} \times \text{Probability of occurrence}} = \text{ROI}$$

Review the following example:

$$\frac{\$10,000 \text{ cost of training}}{\$190,000 \text{ cost of unwanted behavior} \times 10\% \text{ probability of occurrence}} = 53\%$$

This calculation indicates that the cost of targeted training was $10,000. The cost of unwanted behavior to the organization was estimated to be $190,000. Once the targeted training program was delivered, the unwanted behavior would have a recurrence of only 10 percent of the time. The targeted training would immediately save the organization 53 percent of the projected $190,000 that would be lost if the unwanted behavior persisted.

Increasingly, trainers are being asked to demonstrate a return on training investment. Organizations are not willing to approve or continue to fund training and professional development programs unless they are aligned with the strategic and tactical plan and can be cost justified. Providing actual savings and showing a return on training investment can provide the tangible example that justifies the training budget. The key to your success is to design and deliver trainings that are appropriate for all employees so that the skills and knowledge incorporated in the trainings contribute to corporate knowledge and competitive edge.

Summary

Development is the process of creating, testing, and producing usable instructional materials. During the development process, choose instructional strategies that fit the needs of the perspective learners and that are appropriate to the content to be delivered.

Review the instructional strategies and their meaning before you start to construct your training program and develop the learning activities. Use an instructional strategy or peripheral to amplify the learning incident. These strategies should not be integrated into the training design just to provide an activity period, but they should contribute and guide the learning process to achieve an outcome.

Remember to develop a training design report after you've conducted an initial investigation of the problem and found that the identified problem could be resolved with training. The design report is a summary of the work you've completed to date. The report serves three purposes:

1. It is a summary of the analysis results and design work completed thus far.
2. It is a communication tool for key management to ensure that training meets expectations.
3. It is a method for the training manager to supervise the various stages of the design and development of this project.

Calculate the training costs correctly. Use traditional cost accounting principles designed to determine the total cost of training. Once this is done and you've established a measurement mechanism within the training program to measure behavior change, you can then calculate the return-on-investment.

Check-Up Exercise

1. What are the three general categories you use to calculate the true cost of a training program?
2. The ADA protects qualified individuals from unlawful discrimination in the workplace, including access to training and career development. True or false?
3. What is the fair use statement in the Copyright Act of 1976?
4. During the development phase, you select, write, or otherwise obtain all training, documentation, and evaluation materials. List three types of instructional resources you could consider using in your training presentation.

Implementation

Many people think that training of any sort will benefit the organization. Not true. When training is developed without using the steps defined in the training design model, the training event is not always a success.

To make sure that the event is successful, you should be aware that implementation, or delivery, serves as the link between design and development and the training need or opportunity. The reason for this link is that all of the delivery procedures were established during the design stage. Implementation itself carries out the goals and objectives of the program, and it provides the data for assessing program effectiveness. This stage works together with evaluation, which is described in chapter 11.

Prepare the Training Program

People fear making a presentation or speech. The following suggestions will help you develop an effective training presentation:

- ▼ Do your homework.
- ▼ Know your audience.
- ▼ Organize your content.
- ▼ Rely on facts, not opinions.
- ▼ Use examples.
- ▼ Establish high standards.
- ▼ Speak at the audience's level.
- ▼ Treat all trainees as your equals.
- ▼ Answer all questions. (Admit not knowing an answer.)

▼ Think positively.

▼ Exude enthusiasm.

▼ Smile.

Every member of your audience will take away a piece of you, regardless of the type of training you're doing. Although a majority of your audience attended the training because of their interest or need for the knowledge or skill the program provided, the implementation of training—delivery—is what people will remember.

Preparing the training program means identifying your topic, the audience, and the instructional materials. Here are four steps to use for a successful training program.

Step 1: Plan the Presentation

The most essential and time-consuming step is the first one. Planning requires establishing the topic and subtopic areas, understanding the audience's needs, sequencing the topics for logical and easy learning, and building these into the presentation.

Determine the purpose of the training program. Trainers often confuse purpose with objectives so it is important to understand the difference. The training purpose is a single, broadly stated goal, the one result you want your delivery to achieve. (See chapter 8 for an explanation of objectives as they relate to delivery of a training session.) Think of your purpose first in terms of the audience. Remember that your purpose is to effect a change in them. You want them to think or behave differently or to have acquired new knowledge as a result of your presentation. You will determine the purpose on the basis of your needs assessment.

The following are examples of training purposes:

▼ Teach newly promoted managers how to be effective in their roles.

▼ Show technicians how to service the organization's computers.

▼ Illustrate how sales staff can improve customer relations.

▼ Demonstrate computerized reservation systems to new travel agents.

Step 2: Know the Audience

As part of the preparation of your delivery, you must have information about the audience. Every audience, even a training group, has a single, definite personality, regardless of the many personalities and characteristics of individual members. Determine the personality by using the following questions:

▼ Audience Knowledge

— What do they know?

— Have they heard similar presentations?

— Is this topic new to them?

— What is important to learn?

— What do they need to know?

— Are they coming for general knowledge or for specific skills?

— If they are coming to learn specific skills, what kind of skills (for example, job, personal, career, coping)?

— What is not important to learn?

— What do they not need to know?

— How much do they already know about the subject?

— What will they consider superfluous or boring?

▼ Audience Sensitivities

— What should you risk talking about?

— What kinds of backgrounds do they have?

— Is there anything in your background that you could share?

— What topics might insult their beliefs or their intelligence?

— What are their attitudes?

— How can you build credibility?

▼ External Issues

— What time of day is the training?

— What kind of atmosphere exists?

— Will attendees be in a rush to leave at the end?

— Will attendees be drifting in and out during the presentation?

— Are they eager to learn, or are they skeptical about training?

— What are they interested in learning?

— Who is paying for them to attend?

As you proceed through the steps of preparing your delivery, always keep your audience in mind. Neglecting your audience could sabotage the training presentation. You will need to determine the audience's level of knowledge about your topic. Levels will vary greatly. Some members of the audience may know more than you do about particular points, whereas others may not know enough to follow your delivery. An audience's knowledge falls into the following five distinct categories:

▼ no knowledge

▼ below average knowledge

▼ average knowledge

▼ above average knowledge

▼ expert.

Armed with this information, you can now organize your training topic and select an effective instructional strategy that will ensure a successful training outcome. Here are two basic questions to guide your delivery choice:

1. For an informal or general presentation, "What two or three topical points should the audience take away from the event?"
2. For specific skill training, "In which of the five categories does the discerning mind sit?" If you miss the audience knowledge by more than one category, you will not accomplish your training objectives.

If you are unsure about the audience's level of knowledge, be careful.

▼ Do not underestimate the audience's intelligence.
▼ Do not overestimate the audience's knowledge and experience.
▼ Remember, part of knowing your audience is understanding that the audience members want you to succeed.

Step 3: Manage the Physical Setting

Knowing the configuration of the room in which you will be delivering the training is important because you can use the specifics to enhance the presentation. The size and shape of the room, the seating arrangement, and your location relative to that of the audience are critical factors to consider in the preparation phase.

You might ask some of the following questions to become more familiar with the setting:

▼ Is the room properly lighted? You must be able to see the audience, and the audience must be able to see you. Enthusiasm, inspiration, or motivation is almost impossible to communicate in a poorly lit room.
▼ Does the room have cool, fresh air? A room that is too warm and has still air will put your audience to sleep, especially after a meal.
▼ Is the speaking area neat, and does it look professional? The place from which you make your delivery is your personal space, and your audience will judge you by its appearance.

Location

Unless you are lucky, almost all training rooms that you will use were built for something other than training. These room settings range from a traditional classroom setting, a hotel suite, a conference room, a corporate boardroom, a cafeteria, a living room, a multipurpose meeting room, a workshop floor with trolley train axles as your props, to a room in a casino. Make the best of your environment; make the environment work for you.

Furniture

Getting ready to conduct your training might mean moving furniture. Your room setup is not complete without thinking about your training space. It has been discovered recently that the distance trainers stand from the learners affects the degree of warmth, closeness, and, consequently, the level of interaction that will occur between them and the learners. If trainers stand too far from participants, then the presentations tend to take on a formal format; if trainers stand too close, the participants will feel uncomfortable. Be moderate in your approach when starting your event. As time goes by, notice that the learners are establishing a comfortable interaction parameter, and this setting, although unspoken, represents the way you manage the environment. When trainers move freely and frequently, participants perceive that they are knowledgeable, authoritative, and comfortable with the subject matter and the group, and are in complete control. Here are some interesting points that will help you lessen the distance between yourself and the learners:

▼ Stand in front of the room; draw an imaginary line from the learner on your left to the learner on the right; you should be no more than three feet behind the line.

▼ Move all of the comfortable chairs to the front row, thus a reward for sitting up front.

▼ Remove all chairs around the wall and in the back; stack and ship them somewhere so that they cannot be used and distract from the room set up.

▼ If learners have migrated to the back of the room, move the chairs in front and go to them.

Room Setup

Set up the room, if you can. There are six types of setup configurations: classroom, U-shape, conference, circle, small group, and theater. Below is a list of the characteristics of each style to help you make an informed choice about room setup.

Classroom Style. This configuration takes up more space than the theater style and is

▼ good for note taking
▼ good for presentations and delivery of information
▼ not conducive for discussion and group participation
▼ an academic or traditional classroom atmosphere.

U-Shape Style. A U-shaped arrangement is ideal for groups of 10 to 30 people. Everyone can see and interact with everyone else, while attention is focused on you, the speaker. This configuration takes up more room than theater or classroom styles and is

- good for combining the ability to do presentations and hold discussions
- good for note taking
- good for providing a business atmosphere.

Conference Style. This arrangement works for formal and informal meetings of up to 20 people. The conference style is not a preferred style if you want participants to move around the learning environment. A conference style is particularly effective for using visuals and getting focused attention on the presenter. It is

- good for discussion
- good for note taking
- good for presentations
- good for providing a business atmosphere.

Circle Style. This configuration is best for eight to 10 participants. It is good for creating informal and participatory groups and is

- useful for displaying the presenter as a group member or facilitator and less of an authority figure than the other room arrangements
- not good for note taking
- not good for presentations with notes or audiovisual aids.

Small-Group Style. Similar to the U-shaped arrangement, the small group style enables you to walk among your audience. It is

- good when your audience will spend time working or discussing issues
- good for technical presentations, where the goal is to instruct
- good for all types of visual aids.

Theater Style. You will need to ensure that all members of the audience can see you and your visual aids. The theater style is

- good for seating the greatest number of learners in the smallest amount of space
- good and often necessary for groups of more than 50, especially if the room size is limited
- limiting for discussion
- suited to a more formal presentation.

Step 4: Select Materials and Structure

Once you know your audience and the training setting, you are in a better position to select the most appropriate materials and format to use in your presentation. In making selections for all training presentations, you must consider the trainees and the content.

Trainees

When designing the format of your presentation, the most important consideration is the trainees. There are several critical issues to address to ensure that trainees respond to the training and walk away at the end of the program feeling that the program was enjoyable and met their learning needs:

- **Content.** One of the principles of adult learning theory is that adults learn nothing new. Adults merely sort and fit the concepts presented in the training into their existing knowledge base.
- **Motivation.** You do not have the power to motivate anyone to learn. However, you can create environments and opportunities for people to learn by making the training immediately applicable on the job or by ensuring that the training contributes to the trainees' personal and professional growth, or by doing both.
- **Responsibility.** As the trainer, it is your job to help trainees share the responsibility for what it is they are about to learn.
- **Learning skills.** In general, people learn by seeing, listening, or doing. Regardless of the type of learning preference or strategy your trainees possess, all of them learn best when there is a structured lesson plan.

Content

Content is the information, knowledge, or skills you intend to impart. When deciding how to develop the content, first decide whether the presentation should focus on the trainer (trainer centered) or on those being trained (trainee centered). In making this decision, consider the learning outcome, the simplicity or complexity of the content, your skill level as a trainer, and the trainees' level of learning. Table 10-1 displays formats for training programs, according to the focus of the presentation. The left column lists trainer-centered formats in which the trainer is responsible for presentations of theory or skills or is the lecturer. In the right column, there is a list of trainee-centered programs. The middle column lists learning formats that provide learning experiences that represent a partnership in which learners and the trainer take equal roles and responsibilities in the learning process.

Table 10-1. Training formats to match presentations.

Trainer Centered	In Between	Trainee Centered
Theory	Case study	Contract learning
Skills	Role play	Computer-based learning
Lecture	Simulation	Programmed instruction

Contract and computer-based learning and programmed instruction provide the opportunity for learners to assert their control over the content they are to master. These formats let them decide the parameters for learning the content at a time, place, and learning pace.

Trust yourself to know what content is best. You are the authority on your subject even if others don't recognize you as such. You are qualified to speak with authority about experiences and events in your personal and professional life, weaving these experiences and events into your delivery to make points, expand on issues, or use as examples. In doing so, you will put yourself and your audience at ease. In fact, as you collect and select ideas, remember that you are merely having a conversation with your equals, which is what training is.

If after reviewing your notes, you believe your idea generation is a bit weaker than you would like, you can gather additional information through literature searches, personal observations, experiments, surveys, and interviews. Unless your subject is scholarly or extremely technical, you can probably find all the written material you need in books, magazines, and technical manuals. Remember, the key to a memorable training event is that the learners master material and that the training presentation goes smoothly according to the training design.

Tips abound for the best way to organize the materials you have collected and selected. One of the easiest ways to get started putting all the materials together is to write the purpose of the training in large letters on paper and tape it on the wall in

▼▼▼

How do you collect content? One easy way to begin is by jotting down ideas as soon as you know you are going to give a training presentation. To generate more ideas, use brainstorming techniques. Remember that you are simply collecting content. As you select content, you do not need to use every note; you merely need to use the best of the ridiculous or impossible ideas you have noted.

▲▲▲

front of you. Then, create a mental picture of the audience you have identified clearly. Remember that most training presentations have one of two basic purposes: to present information or to develop a skill. Correspondingly, there are two types of training presentations: information oriented (theory) or skill related.

The information-oriented presentation stresses ideas, whereas the skill-related presentation stresses mastery of a particular skill. Often the training topic will dictate which model to apply. At times, however, the training topic will be more ambiguous so that as the trainer, you may consider applying either or both models.

Assume that you were asked to train employees on how to fill out a newly required form. By reviewing the training presentation's objectives (see chapter 8), you may obtain a clearer understanding of which model to use.

Do the trainees only need to learn how to complete the form? Or must the trainees also understand the reason that the new form is being required and how that new form relates to work processes or communication? If the objective is to fill out the form and also to understand the new form's role in work processes, then combine a theory session, in which you explain the role of the form, with a skill session, in which you show how to complete the form.

Theory Session Model

Begin your theory session by presenting background knowledge. The theory session model, as figure 10-1 shows, usually consists of three segments: introduction, body, and closure. First, divide your presentation into these segments, each of which may be relatively independent of one another or may build sequentially upon the other. Each segment needs its own objective.

The introduction is an essential step in setting the tone and direction or intent of the training. Although this is the first part, prepare it last. Remember, you must accomplish the following in your introduction, although you will not have covered some of these points until you have designed and developed the content and selected the appropriate training strategies:

▼ Gain trainees' interest.

▼ Check trainees' current knowledge.

Figure 10-1. Theory session model.

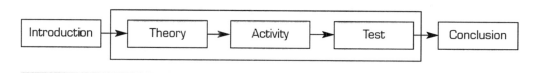

153

▽ Orient trainees.

▽ Preview your material.

▽ Motivate trainees.

You need backup information to support each phase in the body of your presentation: theory, activity, and test. In the body, you must present your major points in logical order.

The conclusion, which briefly reviews the topic and major points, serves three functions:

▽ It links material together.

▽ It clarifies issues.

▽ It ends the presentation.

Time and schedule are important considerations when organizing the presentation. Training programs often have tight schedules, and you must allocate a specific amount of time for presenting a specific amount of information. You must plan to maximize learning per unit of time.

Assume 60 minutes has been allocated for your theory session presentation. You typically have 55 minutes in each hour for your presentation. The introduction and conclusion each take five percent of the time, which would be approximately two and a half minutes each. Divide the remaining 50 minutes not necessarily equally among the body segments. Usually you will spend less time on the theory segment than on the activity and test segments. In the 50-minute presentation, allocate 10 minutes to the theory segment and 20 minutes each to the activity and test segments.

When using the theory session model, you may need to fabricate an activity that facilitates your ability to observe if the trainees have attained the training objective.

Skill Session Model

As figure 10-2 shows, the skill session also has three components. Unlike the body in the theory session, the body in the skill session includes practice.

The introduction in the skill session has three purposes:

▽ Gain trainees' interest.

▽ Check trainees' current knowledge.

▽ Orient trainees.

The body contains three actions:

▽ Show.

▽ Show and tell.

▽ Practice.

Figure 10-2. Skill session model.

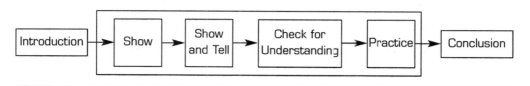

The conclusion serves three functions:

- ▼ It links material together.
- ▼ It clarifies issues.
- ▼ It ends the presentation.

Unlike the theory session model in which you may have to create an activity in which to observe whether trainees have attained the training objective, in the skill session model you readily observe trainees performing the task and applying the content of the session directly. The skill session is all about physical activity (the behavioral component of the objective).

In organizing the skill session, you will break the task down into a series of closely linked steps of physical activity. By having trainees repeatedly practice the steps, you allow them to perform the task more proficiently (measured in terms of time taken and quality of output).

To help you know that you have explained the task successfully, trainees should be able to perform the specified task in less than 10 percent of the total length of the session. Again, using the 55-minute session as an example, trainees have time to learn a five-and-a-half-minute task.

Organize the Presentation

Now that you have established the essential pieces of your training program, you are ready to structure the training event. The training event consists of three sections: introduction of the background and topic; the body of knowledge, theory, or skill; and the conclusion. Let's look at the elements, tips, techniques, and strategies that you need to consider when organizing the training event.

Introduction

You have probably often heard that you get only one chance to make a first impression. This adage holds for your presentation. During your first few sentences, you win or lose your audience. The purpose of your introduction is to open up the trainees' minds so they will be receptive to your delivery and to get the trainees involved immediately in your presentation. In the introduction, tell the audience what the presentation is about and relate the introduction to your overall purpose for giving the presentation. There are several methods you can use in the introduction:

▼ Ask a question.
▼ Make a dramatic statement.
▼ Appeal to a special interest of your audience.
▼ Use visual aids.
▼ Tell a story, anecdote, or personal experience.
▼ Use a quotation.

Body

As you organize the presentation, keep in mind that the body is the development of a statement. A statement can do a variety of things, including the following:

▼ Express an idea.
▼ Make a judgment.
▼ Offer an opinion.
▼ Provide a fact.
▼ Present a matter of inquiry.

You can develop any of these statements through illustration, interpretation, or reinforcement. You can use the following materials to support your development of each statement:

▼ **Fact.** Statistic, data, something that can be proved, such as a typical circumstance or characteristic case to make the statement clear, vivid, and credible.
▼ **Comparison and contrast.** A likeness or difference that associates the new with the familiar.
▼ **Testimony.** The say-so of someone other than you, preferably a well-known authority.
▼ **Quotation.** Type of testimony that is short and to the point. (Note: A testimony is a firsthand verification of a fact; a quotation is a passage in someone's exact words.)

▼▼▼

Remember as you develop the presentation, each major point should be considered a micro presentation with its own introduction, body, and conclusion.

▲▲▲

▼ **Digression.** Built-in element that allows you to act as if you were departing from your script to tell a secret or to relate something that just popped into your head.

▼ **Demonstration.** You perform the action while the audience watches.

▼ **Visual aid.** Laptop computer projected on a screen, 35-mm slides, wall charts or learning maps, 3-D models, or drawings add pizzazz and interest to your presentation, make your points vivid, and help your audience remember the material.

Conclusion

Briefly review your topic and the major points, and provide a summary that states the most important point of the presentation. Here is a list of techniques that assist in summarizing the learning content. You may do one or more of these steps in sequence or simultaneously. Make a choice by considering the topic, the learners' abilities and accomplishments, and the learners' preferences:

▼ Appeal for action by stating what you want the trainees to do.

▼ State your conclusion.

▼ Relate the conclusion to the introduction.

▼ Ask a question.

▼ Use a dynamic quotation.

▼ Stress the relationship of your topic to the trainees' interests.

▼ Pay your audience a compliment.

If you remember only one thing about the conclusion, remember that when you close, close. End your presentation. Make the ending memorable.

Method of Delivery

When thinking about how you will deliver your presentation, remember that you are holding a conversation with your audience. Although at first you might think it would be easier, or at least less frightening, to read or memorize your presentation, if you do, you will not really be engaged in conversation. Imagine the times you have interrupted a direct telephone marketer to ask a question and the person on the other end does not know what to do. Imagine yourself as that person if you were to deliver your presentation by reading or memorizing it.

Read or memorized presentations often sound artificial, and they create unwanted distance between the presenter and the audience. Because you want to effect a change in behavior, you do not want to run the risk of losing your audience. Although it can be helpful to memorize certain sections of your presentation, for example, the introduction and the conclusion, a read or memorized presentation leaves little room for spontaneity or for responding to your audience. In fact, by reading or delivering a memorized presentation, you may be insulting your audience. If that weren't enough to discourage you from reading or memorizing, then think of this: You need to practice long and hard to read well, much longer than practicing to present material as a conversation.

If you are most comfortable reading a presentation, include some of the following extra aids in your script:

▼ colored pens
▼ slash marks to represent places to pause
▼ underlined statements for emphasis
▼ enlarged punctuation marks for exclamation or questions.

Also, enclose passages that you can memorize in boxes so that you can look at your audience when you deliver them. Think of memorization as another form of reading—reading from within. Rather than looking at your notes, you are searching your brain for the information you prepared. Memorization suffers from most of the same disadvantages as reading, especially the inability to maintain eye contact with the trainees.

For the extemporaneous delivery method, you must plan and thoroughly rehearse your presentation and write the presentation as part of your preparation. For an extemporaneous delivery, you do not bring your script, but you do bring notes to serve as reminders of the introduction and conclusion, key statistics, and catch words and phrases that you will use as main points.

Presentation

This is it. Now you must create the presentation you will deliver. Creating a presentation is actually less threatening than writing essays or business reports because no

▼ ▼ ▼

Extemporaneous delivery is best and has some of the following advantages:

- It adapts to a variety of circumstances.
- It encourages audience involvement and interaction.
- It projects spontaneity and enthusiasm regardless of how often you deliver the same presentation.
- It injects interest and enthusiasm.

▲ ▲ ▲

one will review your grammar, punctuation, or spelling. Again, remember that you are writing a conversation. You are creating a lasting impression designed to effect a change in behavior. You are leaving your listeners with memories.

As you write your presentation, be yourself and write in a conversational style as if you were writing a friend a letter. Although you will have everything you need by the time you are ready to sit down to create the presentation, make sure you give yourself more than one day to create it. The longer the training session, the more time you will need to allow for preparing the delivery of the session.

Good presentations are clear and concise, and although they are conversations, the language is more formal than that of ordinary, casual conversations. You must choose your words carefully.

Words

Words can be simple and produce an image of the object named. Use words that are as specific as possible to help your audience see, hear, feel, smell, or taste what you mean. Words also can be complex and have more than one meaning. Sometimes words are misleading, and often they are only close approximations of true meanings.

The following tips may help you choose your words:

▼ **Use familiar words**. In general, familiar words are easier to understand than fancy words. Familiar words tend to be shorter, more concrete, and more vivid.

▼ **Be careful with technical terms and business jargon**. The preparation you did during step 2 will help you limit your words to your audience's level. Even if you believe your audience will understand technical words, do not use them (it is best not to assume anything). Use technical terms and business jargon only when you know every person in the audience will understand the words.

▼ **Use concrete and specific words**. You can help yourself to use concrete and specific words if you use examples or vignettes that a member of the audience provided you during the presentation rather than the canned examples that you use all the time. To do this, you will have to listen carefully and integrate the content and the process of the training that you are facilitating. At times you will want to use abstract concepts, such as justice, good, or profit, rather than specific words. Be sure to clarify the meaning by giving examples or illustrations. Be specific whenever you can. Rather than referring vaguely to a large city in southern California, for example, say San Diego if you mean San Diego or Los Angeles if you mean Los Angeles.

▼ **Use action words**. Use the best action words you can to describe the training. Search, if you must, for action words that suggest movement or convey what they mean either by how they sound or by their imagery. Consider solid words, such as slash rather than cut, shred rather than crumble, and shout rather than say.

▼ **Use figures of speech, such as similes and metaphors**. A simile is a comparison of two things that, in general, are not considered part of the same universe. Similes are introduced by the words *as* or *like*. A metaphor is an implied comparison.

Visual Aids

As you write your presentation, think of how you can use visual aids and incorporate them. Visual materials have several benefits:

▼ arouse interest
▼ encourage participation
▼ prevent misunderstanding
▼ persuade
▼ focus attention
▼ save time
▼ reinforce ideas
▼ add humor
▼ enhance credibility
▼ explain the inaccessible.

Visual materials supplement your presentation. Do not use visual materials as a script, but rather as a checklist of key ideas you will explain, expand upon, and emphasize.

The following are types of visual aids:

▼ **Charts**. Charts can be configured as words, as an organizational structure, as a pie, or as a series of sheets of paper.

— Word charts are lists and tables that you can prepare quickly. When creating word charts, use the seven-seven rule: limit lines of type to seven; limit words per line to seven.

— Organization charts are useful to explain processes and operations.

— Pie charts show percentage distribution, with the circle or pie representing the whole and the segments. When using pie charts, make sure everyone in the audience can see the smallest part. Consider different colors for the segment or segments you want to emphasize.

— Flipcharts are large, blank sheets of paper, bound at the top. The original flipcharts were made from the large sheets of newsprint. Now, another brand of flipchart is available that has a sticky portion at the top back of each page to enable it to adhere to a surface. No more looking for tape to hang those charts on the wall!

▼ **Cutaways**. Cutaways are techniques for showing aspects of the interior of an object in such a way as to clarify the spatial relationships.

▼ **Maps**. Maps should include only the specific features of land or sea that serve the purpose of the presentation. Eliminate elements that do not enhance your purpose.

▼ **Graphs**. Several types of graphs are used commonly:
  — line graphs, which show how related sets of facts change according to a common measure of reference, usually time
  — profile graphs, which present the same sort of information using shadowing or coloring
  — bar graphs, which compare two facts, but do not show how they change over time.

▼ **Projected visual aids**. Computer-generated slides projected from laptop computers are fast becoming the most commonly used visual aid. Other types of projected visual aids are 35-mm slides and overhead transparencies. Projected visual aids are useful for large groups because everyone in the audience can see them. They also give trainers control over the image because they can turn the projector off. Projected visual aids can easily lend themselves to humor and help generate a sense of community among trainees who do not know one another. Following are some rules to keep in mind when using projected visual aids:
  — Illustrate one idea only per slide.
  — Use only 15 words per slide.
  — Make sure the letters are legible.
  — Keep the content simple.
  — Use color whenever possible.
  — Use several consecutive slides to explain complex information.

Most facilities have overhead projectors on hand. Consider using overhead projectors when you want to show the following types of items:

▼ **Transparencies**. Transparencies are easy to photocopy and distribute to the audience after the presentation.

▼▼▼

Flipcharts lose their effectiveness when used for groups of more than 40 people. When using flipcharts, be sure to direct your attention to the audience, not the flipcharts. If you need to improve your handwriting on flipcharts, or even on white boards, practice. Try holding the markers at different angles until you are satisfied that you see some improvement. Experiment with pens and markers. Find the ones that work best for you.

▲▲▲

- ▼ **Text and photos from other sources**. Your daily newspaper often contains the very item that will enhance your presentation. Also, check books and magazines.
- ▼ **Cartoons**. Use cartoons carefully to make sure they do not offend any member of the audience. You can turn an ordinary photograph into a cartoon by adding an incongruous caption.
- ▼ **Models, mockups, and props**. These types of visual aids have high-impact value, but often can be expensive and time-consuming to prepare. The biggest advantage of using models, mockups, and props is that they add realism to your presentation because of their three dimensions.

For the most effective use of any visual aid, keep in mind the following points:

- ▼ **Size and visibility**. The visual aid must be large enough so everyone in the audience can see it clearly and read it easily. Audiences find visual aids that they cannot see annoying and distracting. Instead of paying attention to what the visual aid is communicating, audience members are desperately contorting themselves so as to see the image. To make your visual aids large enough so everyone can see them, you need to know the physical setting in which the training will take place. If you can, experiment with the visual aids in the actual room in which you will be delivering your presentation.
- ▼ **Details**. Details that are not essential to your point can detract from your presentation. Unless decoration is the point you are trying to make, do not be decorative.
- ▼ **Precision**. Make sure your visual aids are neat and precise. Sloppy or careless visual aids reflect poorly on you as a trainer.
- ▼ **Focus**. Remember that your eyes are on the audience, not on the visual aids. The trainees' eyes must be on the visual aids.

Table 10-2. Retention and presentation method.

Presentation method:	Percentage of Information Retained	
	After 3 Hours	After 3 Days
Tell Only	70	10
Show Only	72	20
Show and Tell	85	65

▼ **Introduction.** Every visual aid needs to be put into context. First state what the visual aid is intended to show and then point out its main features.

▼ **Planning.** Incorporate your visual aids into your script, and rehearse them exactly as you plan to present them. Do not show a visual aid until you are ready to talk about it, and as soon as you are finished talking about it, remove it from sight.

Perhaps the most important reason to use visual materials is that people learn more through sight than through any other sense. Visual materials help people retain what they learn. As table 10-2 shows, people retain information longer in presentations that both show and tell. Trainees are likely to remember much more, much longer if you show as well as tell your presentation.

You can help your audience retain what you present by adhering to the KISS and KILL principles:

▼ KISS: Keep It Simple and Succinct

▼ KILL: Keep It Legible and Large.

Editing Tips

After you have completed preparing the presentation, put it away for at least a day. Then come back to the presentation and read it aloud critically. You will be amazed at what reading aloud uncovers. As you read it aloud, you have time to revise the language and sentence structure as more fitting words and phrases come to mind or as you trip over clumsy and unclear sentences.

Learn to be your own harshest critic. By editing your presentation before anyone else has seen it, you can save yourself from an audience of editors and critics, some of whom love nothing more than finding glitches in an expert's presentation.

As you edit, ask yourself the following questions:

- ▼ Does the material fit the purpose?
- ▼ Does the organization follow the objectives?
- ▼ Are the main points properly balanced in terms of presentation time and amount of coverage?
- ▼ Are any points unnecessarily duplicated?
- ▼ Is the presentation written in a conversational style?
- ▼ Does sentence length vary?
- ▼ Do any sentences seem too long?
- ▼ Have you included enough illustrations, examples, comparisons, statistics, and quotes?
- ▼ Will you be able to acknowledge contradictory views and refute them?
- ▼ Are there enough benefits to persuade?

Notes

Even though you have prepared your presentation in every respect, become familiar with your audience and the physical setup, and organized your material, you still must prepare for something to go wrong. Easy-to-follow notes can help you overcome most of the annoying mishaps you are likely to encounter. You must be able to see your notes in bright or dim lights and when you change your position to accommodate visual aids. The following tips can help you prepare your presentation notes:

- ▼ Use a large typeface.
- ▼ Double or triple space between lines, and double that space between paragraphs.
- ▼ Use hanging indents for paragraphs so the first line will be easy to spot.
- ▼ Keep a complete sentence on one page, and whenever possible, keep an entire paragraph on one page.
- ▼ Put six periods at the end of sentences, so you do not run them together accidentally.
- ▼ Type words the way you will say them (for example, one and a half million dollars not $1,500,000).
- ▼ Use only one side of the sheet of paper, and do not fasten the sheets in any way.
- ▼ Number the sheets of paper.
- ▼ Mark where visual aids occur exactly by putting a key word or a sketch in the margin.

Rehearsals

Half of the preparation for your presentation is rehearsal. As the presenter, you are the playwright and the cast. By practicing in as many ways as possible, you will find that you are thoroughly prepared. Consider adhering to the following suggestions:

- ▼ Rehearse enough to learn your presentation and then go through the entire presentation each time you rehearse. If you make a mistake or omit an item, proceed as if you were actually delivering the presentation. This teaches you to deal more easily with mistakes.

- ▼ Reduce relying on your notes more and more as you rehearse. If you can make mental notes of the important points of your introduction and your conclusion, you will have an easier time maintaining continuous eye contact with the audience during these critical parts of the presentation.

- ▼ Practice with a tape recorder. Listen to your voice to hear if it sounds pleasant, lively, and interesting. Do your pace, inflection, and pitch vary, or do you sound monotonous? Does your voice trail off at the end of sentences?

- ▼ Videotape your rehearsal. Check gestures, eye contact, body movement, and how you interact with your visual aids; listen to your voice. Pay attention to repeated mannerisms that may be annoying, such as pushing hair out of your face or saying "you know."

- ▼ Rehearse in front of people. Pay attention to the rehearsal audience's comments, and trust your own opinions. Rehearsing in front of people will help you feel more confident and prepared for your delivery.

- ▼ Practice ad-libbing. If you do not read your script, you will undoubtedly ad-lib. By practicing, you will feel more comfortable during the actual delivery.

- ▼ Dress for a dress rehearsal. Wear what you plan to wear during the delivery, which will help you discover how well your attire will react to movements and gestures. Dress comfortably and appropriately.

Personality

To successfully manage an audience, you must first manage yourself; you are the expert. Use your personality, your nervousness, or your enthusiasm to your advantage. You will discover some things about your personality each time you rehearse. When you think of delivery as an opportunity rather than a frightening prospect, you will have an easier time adopting the following tips:

- ▼ Pretend that you are brave.
- ▼ Focus your attention on the subject of the presentation, and move your mind off yourself.

▼ Convert fear into positive nervousness by accepting rather than resisting fear.

▼ Enjoy yourself, and think of your fears as opportunities.

▼ Avoid stimulants or depressants, such as caffeine or alcohol.

▼ Do isometrics while waiting to give your introduction.

▼ Pay attention to your breathing to ensure you are breathing rhythmically.

Don't let your fear control your delivery. Remember that everything gets easier after you do it several times.

Much of training is preparing to peak at the moment of performance. Athletes prepare physically and mentally for just such moments, and you can do the same. Your attitude more than your ability will win an audience. Employers often select a more enthusiastic candidate, rather than a more qualified one. You can ensure that you'll make a successful delivery by sharing your enthusiasm with your audience. Enthusiasm shows that you believe in yourself and in your subject.

Be careful not to fake enthusiasm. Your audience will sense immediately if you are not being genuine. By accepting and understanding that a warm and spontaneous delivery is better than a perfect one, you will guarantee being naturally enthusiastic. Yes, be dramatic, but appropriately so. Exaggeration is an important and necessary element of oral communication. Remember, most likely you will not have exciting scenery or backdrops for your presentation, so let your personality be some of the scenery.

Success Techniques

If there is an opportunity before you begin your delivery, mingle with your audience projecting a friendly, confident attitude. If there is no such opportunity, see if you can rework the schedule ever so slightly so as to create the opportunity to gather with your audience first.

Once you are introduced as the presenter, walk briskly with purpose and confidence to the speaking position. Immediately connect with your audience, glancing at people with whom you have just mingled. Smile and limit your movements and gestures during the first few minutes of your presentation.

Begin speaking at a low pitch, yet loud enough so as to be heard. Stand about six to eight inches away from the microphone. Even if you are shaking in your shoes or your hands are trembling, keep going and do not pay attention to your feet or your hands. After a few minutes, you will relax and be on your way to a successful delivery.

In general, if you can begin by making a remark or two that directly pertain to your specific audience, you will be telling the audience members that you understand them. If possible, tell them something they did not think you would know about them as a group. As simple as it might sound, your audience will be interested in you if you show you are interested in them.

Be positive and confident, and never apologize or make excuses for anything. For example, the full-service shop that you have relied on to turn your sketches into dynamic visual aids might not have come through as it usually does. Don't reveal this disappointment to your audience.

Delivery is the stage at which everything comes together. Through your knowledge, authority, concern, and confidence, which you communicate through your appearance, gestures, face, eyes, and voice, and the content of your presentation, you will be as good as it gets when it comes to delivery.

Manage the Audience

Now that you have reached your defining moment in the delivery, you are ready to show your stuff. You have planned and organized your presentation, and you have learned about your audience and the physical setting in which you are about to reside temporarily. Here you are engaged in conversation with your trainee group, your equals, and you imagine that everything you have prepared is designed to generate responses. Regardless of the level of perfection you have achieved in your rehearsals, you are never really certain of what kind of reaction or response your delivery will generate. However, because of your rehearsals and your experience and because you are an authority, you will manage the audience successfully. You will adapt to your audience's responses. As members of the audience respond, be confident that you will adjust your delivery, both content and presentation style, accordingly.

But what if your worst fears are realized and your audience seems to be looking around the room and not at you, or worse, what if they seem to be falling asleep? If you recognize this kind of response, risk more not less. Make your delivery more dramatic. Identify a few sympathetic looking faces and play to them. Communicate an increased level of caring about your audience.

If you sense that there might be a problem, ask the audience members to share their concern or discuss the situation with you. It is best to clarify an issue or problem, not to ignore it. It's best for everyone concerned that you know what's going on: best for the learners to know that you know that they know and that you want to understand and engage in problem solving the situation!

One sure method for managing the audience is to use the SEE factor:

▼ **Spontaneity.** Respond immediately to issues of concern or concepts that need clarification.

▼ **Enthusiasm**. Be genuinely glad to be facilitating the learning situation; welcome their questions or queries. If the issue is not appropriate when it is presented, agree on a mutual time or forum for discussion.

▼ **Eye contact**. Be an active listener by looking at the person talking with you, and be an active presenter by focusing on the members of your audience. Don't look over their heads or at your notes, the flipcharts, or the visual aids: talk to them. Be engaging.

Teaching is holding a conversation. Provide a structure for the conversation and direct the dialogue so that it is open and satisfying for the learners and for you, the trainer.

Watch Your Time

Your time limit is a contract between you and your audience. The two most important clauses of the contract are starting on time and ending on time.

When you were planning, preparing, and rehearsing your presentation, you paid attention to time. More than likely you devoted appropriate time to each segment. When you plan for one full day or more, be realistic about your timing. Design in minutes for each hour. Five minutes within each 60 minutes is for the learners to settle in. There are six hours of training time per day, not eight. And there are breaks! We are now discovering in learning–brain research that learners need to take mental breaks every 20 minutes and physical breaks every 50 minutes. Allocate your time according to your major points.

When you are making your delivery, trust yourself. If the time allocation does not seem appropriate as you proceed in your presentation, make adjustments.

Plan the Question-and-Answer Session

Most presentations build a question-and-answer session into the end. This session allows the conversation you are having to move in directions the trainees might want to go. Plan ahead by having answers to questions that your various rehearsal audiences might have asked or that you anticipate this audience might ask.

What do you do if the unthinkable happens, and no one is asking a question? You have several options:

▼ You can avoid the appearance of no questions by planting a colleague or two in the audience who will ask questions. Sometimes that one question will encourage other people to start asking.

▼ You can ask a question yourself: "Someone once asked me. . . ."

▼ You can end the presentation gracefully: "Seeing that there are no questions, let's end for today."

Audiences have a variety of reasons for asking questions. Don't assume that all those who ask questions are seeking information. People may ask questions to test you, show their own knowledge, make points, or get your approval. Your ability to manage questions and questioners is important to the success of your delivery. Following are some tips for managing your audience during the question-and-answer session:

▼ Receive all questions in an open, friendly manner. Don't react or be defensive, even if someone is trying to put you on the spot.

▼ Listen carefully and restate the question to make sure you understand it and the entire audience hears it.

▼ Think before you answer. Consider the following processing points before providing a response:

— Why is someone asking this question?

— How does this question fit with my purpose?

— How can I answer as briefly and as well as possible?

Use the KISS principle. However, do not answer simply yes or no; answer with a short, to-the-point statement, perhaps supported by a brief example. Admit to not knowing an answer, and offer to find out the answer and then follow up with the answer.

Close With Conviction

Use body language to indicate that you have finished your presentation. Nod, and step back briskly from your speaking position.

Merely saying, "Thank you," is too short and too often reveals the unspoken and felt, "Thank God that's over." Use SEE—spontaneity, enthusiasm, and eye contact—especially enthusiasm, to help you close with conviction. You might close with words such as, "I enjoyed being with you. Thank you for your attention and your participation. Best of luck to all of you."

Exit a Winner

When you are planning, organizing, and rehearsing your presentation, be sure to include how you will leave the speaking area as well as what you will do immediately upon leaving the area. You have several options:

▼ to sit in the chair from which you were introduced

▼ to stand on stage to greet people

▼ to move around the room to greet people

▼ to go into the hall to greet people

▼ to leave the area so that the group can proceed to another activity.

You want to manage your audience in the last moment the same way you managed them in the first moment and throughout the delivery: professionally. Leave the way you entered: briskly, firmly, and confidently. Remember that although you may no longer be holding a conversation, you are "on" until you are out of sight.

Summary

Following are key points to remember when you prepare to implement your presentation:

- ▼ Delivery is holding a conversation with your audience.
- ▼ The most important and time-consuming step is planning the delivery.
- ▼ Conduct research to help you know your audience and the venue in which you will be making your presentation.
- ▼ Selecting materials and the format for your delivery requires understanding the relationship of your content to the type of training you will be conducting.
- ▼ Organizing the presentation forces you to decide whether you will use the theory session or the skill session model and to plan the body, the conclusion, and the introduction in that order.
- ▼ Creating the presentation provides the opportunity to think about what words you will use, what type of visual aids will best support your words and your message, how to benefit from editing your script and rehearsing your presentation, and how to put the best of your personality into your presentation.
- ▼ Create effective visual aids:
  — Use large type or letters.
  — Write clearly.
  — Limit the number of ideas per chart and focus on key words or ideas.
  — Remember the seven-seven rule.
  — Explain, amplify, or give examples of the words on the visual aid.
  — Use a progression technique—expose one idea at a time—for particularly complicated visual aids.
- ▼ Managing your audience is merely paying attention to the group with whom you are engaged in conversation, which is best done by fulfilling your contract to deliver on time and in the allotted time.

Use the presentation checklist in table 10-3 to check off each stage of the presentation as you complete it.

Consider monitoring the progress of your presentation by summarizing questions or creating a checklist on a flipchart or learning map that depicts the major elements of the presentation. If you use a wall chart or learning map, make sure you refer to each element on it. If you use a visual checklist, make sure you check off the segments you complete. The presentation checklist is for you to keep track of your

Table 10-3. Presentation checklist.

Item	Date Completed
Accept invitation to deliver training.	
Write the title.	
Determine the purpose.	
Prepare the instructional objectives.	
Identify your audience.	
Learn about the physical setting in which you will deliver training.	
Research the content.	
Organize your material and determine the exact content.	
Plan the body.	
Plan the conclusion.	
Plan the introduction.	
Decide which delivery method you will use.	
Create the presentation.	
Plan the visual aids.	
Engage a full-service shop to execute the visual aids.	
Receive professionally prepared visual aids.	
Type your notes.	
Rehearse for yourself.	
Rehearse for others.	
Conduct a dress rehearsal.	

topic and your timing. Develop a mechanism that works best for you. You can share your checklist with the audience if you so choose. Remember the following rules:

- ▼ Write talking notes in pencil.
- ▼ Change colors in your talking notes for visual interest and relief.
- ▼ Underline your talking notes for clarity.
- ▼ Underline your talking notes for emphasis.

Check-Up Exercise

1. What is the KISS method?
2. In organizing the skill session, you will break the task down into a series of closely linked steps of physical activity. What are the elements that you would use?
3. What are two ways you can monitor your presentation summary?

Evaluation

Evaluation is closely entwined with implementation. But before you can deliver the training program, you need a plan to deliver the training and evaluate its effect on the learners.

Training should be a part of an integrated system in which performance is measured against criteria (best-practices benchmarks) that are tied to the overall organizational strategic objectives and the learning objectives.

A training program is organized around three phases of learning. Each phase provides an opportunity for you to evaluate effectiveness and learner outcome.

▼ Phase 1: Setting the Stage for Learning
— Provide clear task instructions.
— Model appropriate behavior.
— Communicate management support.

▼ Phase 2: Increasing Learning During Training
— Provide for active participation.
— Match training techniques to trainees' abilities.
— Provide opportunities for mastery practice.
— Ensure specific, timely, diagnostic, and practical feedback.

▼ Phase 3: Maintaining Performance After Training
— Develop learning points to assist in knowledge retention.
— Set specific goals.
— Identify appropriate reinforcers.
— Train others in how to reinforce behavior.
— Teach self-management skills to trainees.

During training, take the needed steps to increase knowledge and skill retention and conclude the training event with specific evaluation strategies to provide learners opportunities to think through how they can transfer the training successfully to the job.

How well management supports the learners and the instructor has an effect on training. If management does not encourage course participation and follow-up on the job, then training will not succeed. Training will succeed if management acts as a visible and vocal sponsor for the training, the instructor, and the training process to support training job skills transfer.

Evaluate the Return-on-Investment

Evaluation allows you to determine the effectiveness and efficiency of your training program. The purpose of evaluation is to

- determine if training is meeting its stated goals and objectives
- determine if the implementation of the training program is practical
- determine if the learners are meeting established performance criteria
- provide necessary feedback so that the training program can be maintained.

Evaluation is a vital part of any training program. Evaluation is a significant part of the instructional design and delivery process, not just an element in program outcomes. As part of the program development process, evaluation can help programs succeed and can stop ill-conceived or poorly executed programs from happening.

It is important to plan the evaluation process early in the design stage to establish the mechanisms for assessing the ongoing effect of the training, rather than to wait to assess the effect after program delivery. Consider using the following five-step evaluation strategy to adequately separate knowledge and skills assessment. By assessing skills separate from knowledge, you are better able to design appropriate re-training to target a specific need. The five levels are as follows:

1. **Self**. As a trainer, you need feedback. Trainers often overlook the need to conduct self-analysis feedback, but you need to take the time to reflect on your performance, to ask yourself what went well, what did not go so well, and what you might need to change. In addition to your own insight, you can receive feedback from trainees' evaluation forms and colleagues' feedback. Questions you could use in any of the situations to start a dialogue include "Could I have done better?" and "What are areas for improvement?"

2. **Course materials**. The materials are usually designed in a one-dimensional, written format. You don't know how the written notes and suggested processes

are going to evolve until the training takes place. Therefore, the learners' comments, written trainees' evaluation critiques, and your observations in the training session provide you with the needed feedback. Questions include "Does the material work?" "Are there portions that are difficult to deliver?" "Do learners exhibit difficulty with materials or training situations?" and "Do courses or training processes need revising or updating?"

3. **Course curriculum**. Like the course materials, the course curriculum is prepared on paper. The implementation phase allows you to test your design by getting feedback during the training delivery process. Your feedback would, therefore, come from yourself, learners, or observers. Questions include "Does the course curriculum hang together?" and "Does the course meet the intended learning objectives and outcomes?"

4. **Course modules**. Just as with the course materials and course design, the course modules are your written interpretation of what you should deliver. Your feedback consists of a self-analysis of the course modules, your experience during the delivery stage, and the reactions from learners or observers. Questions include "Are the modules organized around a theoretical theme?" "Are the topics sequenced in logical order?" and "Does each module contribute to the course outcomes and learning objectives?"

5. **Learning transfer**. Both written and oral feedback about the transfer of learning to the workplace are important during the training event and as a post-training activity. Questions include "How effective was the transfer of learning to each learner's work situation?" and "How effective is the learning transfer to the real world of work?"

Types of Evaluation Design

There are various types of evaluation designs. Collection of data varies to suit different needs based on the details of a training.

One-Shot Program Design

The one-shot program design for evaluation of a single group after completion of a training program collects no data prior to the program. Many uncontrolled factors, such as the environment (time of day and place) and the trainees' attitudes (energy level, accomplishments, perceived ability to transfer the learned concepts and thoughts about the training) might influence the design's measurement and invalidate conclusions drawn from it.

There are two situations in which this design may be useful: when measuring the performance of a group for which it was not possible to measure performance beforehand and when there is no significant knowledge, skill, or ability existing before the program is conducted.

Single-Group Pretest and Posttest Design

The single-group pretest and posttest design goes one step beyond the one-shot program design by collecting data before and after the training program. To detect improvements, the learners' knowledge, skills, or abilities before the program are compared with their knowledge, skills, or abilities after the program. The disadvantage of the pretest strategy is that it may sensitize learners to the training content, which might affect the posttest.

Single-Group Time Series Design

A single-group time series design is a series of measurements for evaluating training programs before and after the program. In this design, the experimental group serves as its own control group. The multiple measurements prior to the program eliminate the problems incurred when a separate control group is not used. Repeated measurements after the program allow for comparison of the initial results and enable measurement of the program's long-term effect.

Control Group Design

The control group design compares two groups, one experimental and one control. The experimental group receives the training program, whereas the control group does not. Data is gathered on both groups before and after the program. Comparing the results of the experimental group to the control group assesses the effect of the training program. For this design to be acceptable, the two groups must be similar with respect to the selection criteria.

Decisions Around Evaluation

An effective evaluation is essential to improve a program and demonstrate its value. One of the important considerations is when to evaluate. The evaluation and feedback process is necessary to ensure that the activities are directly related to the needs of the learners or decision makers. Evaluations assess both the outcomes of the training program and the components of instructional design and development.

Silberman and Lawson (1995) suggest that evaluation efforts should address what is happening in a training program and the possible effects on learning and the participants. He suggests an evaluation process that involves inquiry and decision making throughout the design and development processes. Silberman suggests making decisions in the following areas:

▼ **The elements to be evaluated.** Data can be gathered concerning any of the following elements: program content and design; trainer's competence; learners' knowledge, skills and attitudes; training facilities; and organizational results.

▼ **The tools to be used to collect evaluative data.** They may include questionnaires, observation, tests, reports, and interviews.

▼ **The timing for data collection.** Data collection may occur during pretraining, training, the end of training, and the follow-up period.

Types of Evaluation

There are two types of evaluation processes for measuring a training program's effectiveness: formative and summative.

Formative evaluation activities occur throughout the business justification, analysis, design, development, and implementation stages to identify required revisions.

Summative evaluation activities occur at the end of training program delivery to determine if the training met the goals and objectives. Summative evaluation can include performance-based evaluation, follow-up or longitudinal evaluation, and program effectiveness evaluation.

Table 11-1 can assist you in deciding which evaluation process you should use to measure program effectiveness. When you conduct a program evaluation, keep in mind that a good quality evaluation consists of a comprehensive data-collection effort and a consistent and conscientious attempt to revise instructional materials on the basis of these data.

Table 11-1. Types of evaluation processes.

Type	Description	Method
Formative	Type of evaluation that assesses the program before full implementation. Instructional designer usually conducts with small focus groups.	Test materials and instructional methods at each phase of the development.
Summative	Type of evaluation that assesses the final training program or product after implementation (usually with Kirkpatrick's levels model).	Determine degree to which objectives were met and the results after widespread use of training.

Types of Measurement

There are four basic tactics for measuring results: experimental, critical incident, problem solving, and management information system.

The experimental approach emphasizes comparing trained and untrained, or pre- and post-trained learners (or some combination of both) on several predetermined measures of performance. After a reasonable period of time, the results are compared by using a descriptive statistical process. Because there are so many possible variables, both positive and negative correlations can occur by chance, especially if only a single outcome is being measured. The consequence is that you can't necessarily rely on statistical results to prove your program's effect.

The critical incident approach requires the trainer to solicit and collect specific incidents of improved performance from the trained population to show the effectiveness of the training effort. With this approach, a lot of evaluative information is generated, and if done in a systematic and logical way, you can continuously tie results to program objectives.

With the problem-solving approach, the trainer is involved in identifying, quantifying, and solving high-priority problems, and the contribution to profits is easily measured. High-priority problems easily lend themselves to pre- and postmeasurement and provide high visibility. If training programs are based on clear objectives that have been developed by careful needs analysis and are directly related to profit-producing performance, then the results of training will invariably be quantifiable.

The management information system approach holds that looking at the effect of training should be part of an ongoing performance tracking and feedback system. Tracking and feedback should include attitude, after-training performance, and ongoing progress reports.

Training Transfer Evaluation

Transfer of training is the effective and continuing on-the-job application of knowledge and skills gained in training—both on and off the job, according to Broad and Newstrom (1992). Although learning is the planned outcome of any training, the most important critical event for any training is to have the learner transfer the new skills, knowledge, and abilities to the job.

Learning transfer can occur in a variety of ways. Donald L. Kirkpatrick (Kirkpatrick & Kirkpatrick, 2006) developed one of the most popular models. Table 11-2 describes the levels, the types of evaluation, and the key questions. He identifies the following four levels at which training can be evaluated:

▼ Level 1, reaction (attitude or feeling regarding satisfaction and dissatisfaction with the training)

Table 11-2. Evaluating successful training transfer.

Level	Evaluates	Description
1	Reaction	How did the learner react to the course?
2	Learning	How well did the learner apply the new skills and knowledge during the course?
3	Behavior	What changes in job behavior resulted from the training?
4	Results	What were the results of training on the company's bottom line?

Source: Donald L. Kirkpatrick and James D. Kirkpatrick, *Evaluating Training Programs: The Four Levels*, 3d.ed. (San Francisco: Berrett-Koehler, 2006).

- ▼ Level 2, learning (observable or measurable behavior change in the classroom or training situation)
- ▼ Level 3, behavior (new or changed behavior, performance back on the job)
- ▼ Level 4, results (for example, increased productivity, sales quality, or reduction in costs, accidents, grievances due to appropriate training that addressed the identified need).

At Level 1, you evaluate a learner's reaction. Reaction sheets, or happy sheets, are the most popular mechanism for conducting this evaluation. This evaluation only measures how a person feels about the training, that is, happy or not happy.

At Level 2, you evaluate a learner's mastery of the program content by using a test. This evaluation only measures the learner's ability to answer test questions.

At Level 3, you evaluate a learner's ability to transfer the learning on the job. This evaluation is difficult to accomplish unless you have had prior discussions with the learner's supervisor, and he or she agreed that certain mastery should occur in the learning and that the successful transfer of the training will be reported.

At Level 4, you evaluate the results of the training. This evaluation can only be accomplished if a well-defined training issue that affected the organization was identified and the training targeted the issue.

But how do you get from the four levels of evaluation to designing and conducting the course? Let's consider evaluation methods. Table 11-3 shows when to measure, what to measure, and how to measure for successful learning transfer. The premise of

Kirkpatrick's evaluation model is that these four levels can be used to design and test how successful you were in presenting the information for the learners to master. In the role of the trainer, however, you can only manage and test successful transfer at Levels 1 and 2. Once you begin to assess the success of learning transfer at Level 3, you must include the learner's supervisor. When you want to test the level of successful transfer at Level 4, you first must start with a well-defined needs assessment statement, which defines a need that has a significant effect on the organization and shows training as the solution to the defined need. Once the training has occurred, you can test to determine the effect training had on that need.

To measure how well trainees absorbed material covered in your training program, take advantage of a variety of assessment tools. The most effective assessment methods are checklists, questionnaires, and interviews.

Checklists allow trainers, managers, and trainees to assign value to different training topics. The disadvantage of checklists is that answers are subjective, and, as such, not necessarily valid.

Questionnaires are used when evaluation time is limited and cost is a primary concern. Questionnaires can reach a large number of people and can investigate levels of knowledge, analyze skills, and elicit attitudes. Properly formatted questionnaires provide data for relatively easy statistical analysis. The disadvantages are that responses are subjective, there are difficulties constructing easy-to-understand questions, and there are problems trying to produce a valid and reliable format.

Interviews can be used with trainers, managers, and learners. The interview process can elicit information such as personal impressions about the quality of training and differences in performance. The disadvantages are that interviews are often time consuming and expensive to design, conduct, and analyze.

Table 11-4 shows the advantages and disadvantages of a variety of evaluation methods.

Methods to Measure Behavior

Changes in behavior can be evaluated using a variety of methods. Combining the methods may yield the truest picture of behavioral changes. Methods for evaluating behavior include performance tests, critical incidents, multi-rater 360 feedback, simulations, observations, and performance appraisals.

Performance tests contain actual samples of content taught in the training program. This type of test measures behavior changes that transfer to the work environment.

Critical incidents record significant positive and negative incidents to measure training outcome. An employee's supervisor usually conducts this evaluation. The

Table 11-3. Evaluation worksheet.

Level	When to Measure	What to Measure	Measure Used Instrument
1	During program (end of day) End of program	Reactions Pace and sequence Relevance (content) Instrument strategies Interaction Facilitator's style Level of discussion Objectives met Environment Knowledge of facilitator Participant interaction Registration process	Questionnaire Individual response in class Follow-up interviews
2	During the program Pre and post (end)	Is learning taking place, and to what extent? Teaching of content Knowledge of participants	Knowledge tests Performance tests, role plays, case studies Checklists Product tests
3	After the program A few weeks to three months	On-the-job change	Performance records Performance contracts Action plans Interviews Observation with checklists
4	After the program Three months to one year	Impact on organization	Action plans Interviews Questionnaires Focus groups Performance contract
5	After the program Three months to one year	Determine monetary value of impact	Control groups Trend line Participants' estimates Supervisors' estimates Management's estimate Use of experts Extant data External studies

Source: Adapted with permission from Donald V. McCain, Ed.D., Performance Advantage Group, Brentwood, TN.

Table 11-4. Guidelines for evaluating learning.

Strategies	Advantages	Disadvantages
Written tests/assessments (could be pre/post)	• Provides documentation • Immediate feedback • Knowledge reinforcement • Easy to administer • Flexibility in timing • Advanced organizer • Reinforces knowledge content	• Creates anxiety/stress • Difficult to construct • Legal implications
Performance tests/assessments	• Allows for self-discovery • Allows for application • Can be an instructional strategy (case study, role play, etc.) • Reinforces course content and skills • Immediate feedback • Behaviorally oriented • Simulates the job	• Requires time • Legal implications • Training of observers/ assessors • More can affect performance than training (pretraining skills)
Skill tests/ assessments	• Replicates the job • Separates levels of dexterity • Supports job standards • Immediate feedback • Allows for direct application of knowledge and skills • Reinforces skills	• Determining level of performance • Legal implications • Availability of equipment • Availability of room • Training of observers/ assessors
Work product test/assessment	• Replicates the job • Allows for direct application of knowledge and skills • Links to field supervisors/ leads • Supports job/product standards • Subject matter expert involvement • Reinforces skills	• Availability of equipment • Disruptive to work environment • High visibility/Higher risk • Legal implications • Time consuming • May take equipment out of service, impacting production • Training of observers/ assessors • May be difficult to construct and assess

Source: Adapted with permission from Donald V. McCain, Ed.D., Performance Advantage Group, Brentwood, TN.

method measures positive and negative behaviors well, but midrange behaviors are difficult to quantify.

Multi-rater 360 feedback evaluates performance using self, peers, direct reports, management, and other relevant perspectives, such as those of customers and suppliers. The 360-feedback process can involve a multiple-customer approach. Traditional performance management systems focused on one-way feedback: supervisor to employee. Business initiatives, such as total quality management, teams, and reengineering, have resulted in an additional focus on customers and added value. In response to these needs, many organizations have implemented 360-feedback systems, although other organizations have reservations about these systems. One criticism is that the process involves more people and takes more time and money to execute than most other evaluation methods. Critics also say that people rating the employee may not understand the total job requirements and environment. In addition, some critics say that the potential benefits of 360-feedback systems are still unproven.

Keep in mind, however, that when multi-rater systems are well implemented, they provide feedback to the employees from the supervisors, peers, direct reports, and customers (internal and external). When such systems are based upon core competencies, they ultimately support the vision and values of the organization and the changing shape of the organization, the expectations of employees, and the increasing level in interdependence throughout the organization to achieve desired goals.

Simulations provide an experiential bridge between training and its real-world context. How well the trainee performs the simulation can be a measurement of training effectiveness. Simulations that reflect the work environment accurately can be expensive to construct.

Observations assess complex performances that are difficult to assess by means of questionnaires, interviews, or simulations. A problem with this technique is that it must be properly structured for quantitative data collection. An observation checklist is organized to list categories and frequency of behavior to be observed. The checklist becomes the instrument used to help quantify performance.

Performance appraisals evaluate how well employees measure up to various performance standards. During a performance appraisal, the supervisor compares the actual performance to the performance standards and judges whether skills taught in training are practiced in the workshop.

Progress toward organizational objectives will tell management whether training is working well. Training should advance the company toward its mission. If the bottom line is improving, management may approve more funding for training. If the company isn't closer to meeting its objectives, training may be viewed as ineffective.

Evaluation Effectiveness

For evaluation to be effective, several things must be present:

▼ Evaluation must be linked to the needs analysis to determine present and anticipated problems and opportunities.

▼ The feedback must be timely. The evaluation data must be given to the appropriate people while the training program and potential problems are still current.

▼ Evaluation data must be collected on an ongoing basis throughout the training process, summarized right after the training, and acted upon immediately.

▼ The training environment must support change. The effectiveness of an evaluation system is contingent upon a training environment that allows change. An environment not supportive of change could result in a situation in which trainers are not obligated to improve training.

Ongoing data collection is essential for ensuring evaluation effectiveness. The data document changes in performance, instructors' effectiveness, learning, and the like. Interviews, observations, questionnaires, and tests provide information you use in establishing a benchmark with which to make design decisions. This benchmark can then provide the basis for a discussion with management about the need for a training.

Once you collect your information and share it with management, management must then decide on the value of the training. Trainers and the instructional designer should help in interpreting the data by suggesting ways to correct any problems that turn up in the performance study.

There are two basic kinds or categories of data, hard and soft. The primary measurement of improvement is hard data, which is presented as rational, undisputed facts. The ultimate criteria for measuring the effectiveness of management rest on hard data items such as return-on-investment, productivity, profitability, cost control, and quality control. Because changes in the data lag behind changes in the condition of the human organization, it is very useful to supplement these measures with interim assessments of attitude, motivation, satisfaction, and skills. These soft data items are more difficult to collect and analyze but are used when hard data is not available.

There are three basic models for data collection: pre-experimental, true experimental, and quasi-experimental.

1. The pre-experimental model doesn't adhere to the tenants of basic experimental design. A common example is an evaluation that consists of only one group that participated in a training program and then was evaluated without being compared with another group. One way to improve the method would be to test learners before and after the training program, because that would reduce

one source of possible evaluation error. There remains the problem of attributing to the training program the results of the test. The single-group posttest only and the single-group pretest are both considered pre-experimental models.

2. True experimental models have a comparison group that is equivalent to the training group because each person is assigned to a group by a random process. Random assignment increases the probability that the groups are equivalent in every way except that only one group participates in the training program. The problem with implementing a true experimental model is the difficulty with random assignment and the problem of withholding the instruction from the comparison group.

3. The quasi-experimental designs differ from the true experimental designs in that they don't have random assignment to the training group and comparison groups. One commonly used quasi-experimental model has two groups that are not assigned at random, but that are constituted to be as close as feasible. Another possible quasi-experimental model uses multiple measures on one group over time. In this approach, the evaluator takes several performance measures before the training program begins, and then takes several measures after its completion and examines the data for trends.

Data-collection information must be valid and reliable, which requires sound development and use of the instruments. According to Jack Phillips (1997), there are four ways to determine if an instrument is valid: content, construct, concurrent, and predictive validity.

1. The extent to which the instrument represents the content of the program is content validity. Low-content validity means the instrument does not represent a true summation of the program content. High-content validity means the instrument represents a good balance of all the program content.

2. Construct validity refers to the degree to which an instrument represents the construct it is supposed to measure. The abstract variable that the instrument is intended to measure, such as the skill, attitude, or ability, is the construct. Construct validity can be defended through expert opinion, correlations, logical deductions, and criterion group studies.

3. Concurrent validity is the extent to which an instrument agrees with the results of other instruments administered at approximately the same time to measure the same characteristics.

4. The extent to which an instrument can predict future behaviors or results is predictive validity.

A reliable survey instrument is one that is consistent enough that subsequent measurements of an item give approximately the same results. A test or survey is considered reliable if it yields consistent results at two points in time. This assumes that there have been no major changes in people or circumstances and no intervening treatments.

Revise the Program

During the design and development process, check the program objectives and test items that you prepared as a first step in this instructional training system process. Remember, the training system model establishes the blueprint for the design and development of your training. The model dictates the sequential steps involved in developing and evaluating your training.

Evaluation results usually indicate the area to be revised. In a majority of the cases, most revisions surface in the area of timing, content, activities, or course materials. The materials may be handouts, participant workbooks, overheads, or wall charts. Once you've identified one or more areas to be revised, review the training system model and check your data against the step in the model where the deficiency occurs; you do not have to revise your entire training program, just the step that indicates a problem exists.

If an objective statement is faulty, the revision would start at the analysis stage. Or, the trainer might suggest that the content covered in the training program or that the activities that were designed and developed to meet the learning objective need to be addressed to meet the learners' needs or, more specifically, the defined learning outcome. If a module is poorly organized, then the revision starts at the development stage. In many cases, evaluation will include an analysis of end users' interaction with newly learned skills.

To test the effectiveness of training, such as the use of a job aid, observe how well users can perform selected tasks. By conducting this step, you can provide valuable feedback to the training designer. For example, users' problems may reflect a poorly designed software interface rather than a poorly designed job aid.

In these situations, the ultimate goal is to use the evaluation process as a vehicle to identify how the software may be improved, thereby reducing or eliminating the need for training.

Review the Final Program With Management

After the program's outcomes have been clearly delineated, it is important to design a system that will monitor the results achieved both in qualitative and quantitative terms. The outcomes to be tracked are to be mutually agreed upon by the client and the trainer. The system must then tackle both on-the-job behavior change and bottom-line effect to the organization.

Summary

The evaluation provides feedback to the trainer and to the learners. It allows you to determine the effectiveness and efficiency of your training program through the design and delivery stages. Though there are many types of evaluations to choose from, depending on the goal of the training, there will always be a best type of evaluation. Therefore, even though evaluations often occur at the end of the training, they should be considered when the training is being designed.

Check-Up Exercise

1. What are the four reasons to evaluate a training program?
2. When you are working on the design and development process, should you continually check back to determine if the program objectives and test items are appropriate?
3. Does the training system model establish a blueprint for the design and development of your training?

▼ **Part III**

Designing Tips

Tool Kit:
Tips and Techniques

Chapter 5 introduced you to the training system model (see figure 5-1). This tool of the trade is a step-by-step guide for designing and developing successful trainings. By taking training one step at a time, the trainer or designer can ensure that the training is appropriately designed and meets the need of the learners and the sponsoring organization.

Tip 1. Consulting and Contracting

Being a training consultant is not just a title. You are a business. Being in the training business requires planning, marketing, and financial management. Being a professional training consultant means that you are in this business full time, not just until you can find a so-called real job. Training consulting is a real job, and, generally speaking, running a training business is more demanding than many other so-called real jobs.

Tips on Consulting

Before you begin your consulting business, examine the market around you. Determine if the industry has a need for your services and if it is willing to pay for you to perform a service that you can provide. At first, you'll probably perform a variety of duties until you decide that you have found a niche. Finally, finding your niche takes time, research, thought, marketing, and trial and error. Eventually you will carve a market share for your business.

Realistic evaluation of your ability to reach potential customers is important. Having a network of people is critical if you expect an adequate income. You need to be self-directed and disciplined. Each day you must do work—making a client contact, developing a client, and working on a project or on self-development. No day should be a vacation day.

Self-Management

If you are just beginning as a consultant, you should have an adequate income to carry you through the first year or two so you can survive on your own without counting on winning a big contract. If you don't have that kind of income, get yourself an adequate financial cushion. You can't be truly effective in your new business if you are constantly worried about money and making payments each month.

Consulting Cycle

The consulting cycle is simple to understand. You make a presentation to a potential client. You negotiate the fees and arrangements for payment. You perform the service, and you submit an invoice.

Consultant Tips

It takes the following skills and attributes to be a successful training consultant:

- specific, valuable experience and expertise
- ability to make sales calls and manage the sales process
- good telephone skills
- good people skills
- good organizer of time
- self-starter (every day)
- ability to handle finances
- flexibility
- belief in self
- contacts
- comfortable working alone
- patience and respect for all points of view
- ability to know when to seek advice and accept help
- business and market sense
- code of ethics.

Contracting Tips

Here is a checklist of events and activities that you should review before you meet your client or conduct a personal survey activity over the telephone:

1. **Client's needs**: Talk with the client to determine what is needed and wanted. Also determine the following through discussions with the client or your own observations: the client or company norms, the mission of the organization, and the backgrounds of the perspective learners.

2. **Time constraints**: Determine the number of training days, typical training schedule, beginning and ending times, and lunch arrangements. Also discuss the spacing of training days and the pacing of material.

3. **Location**: Suggest that training take place at a neutral location away from the office and telephones. Prior to training, visit the site and look at the physical setup, equipment, and comfort of the proposed meeting site. Also, check the room layout to be sure it suits your needs.

4. **Trainees' roles and experience**: Determine the roles on the job and what previous training programs learners have attended.

5. **Trainer's roles**: Establish the trainer's role and responsibilities. Also, be sure trainers have access to key stakeholders in the organization.

6. **Group size**: Determine the size of the group and decide the method you will use to create work groups and learning communities within the training event.

7. **Opportunity for follow-up**: Establish if there is a chance to meet with the learners and the organization to measure the return-on-investment of the training time and dollars.

During the contract meeting, you go through three stages:

1. **Opening**: In your introduction, establish the need for the meeting. You might also want to develop an agenda for everyone to follow.

2. **Body**: In this stage, present your findings and determine whether the client's interest or needs match your portfolio of skills (and interests).

3. **Closing**: Summarize the important things that you provide the client. Make sure you have a power close.

Tip 2. Responding to a Training Request

A major portion of your training design time will be devoted to requests that you receive from managers. Figure TK-1 shows the steps that the trainer goes through when investigating and responding to a training request.

Tip 3. Designing Training Programs With a Team

When a training staff works together to design a program, it must achieve a high level of efficiency and creativity. If the staff members for a training program are new

Figure TK-1. Flow chart.

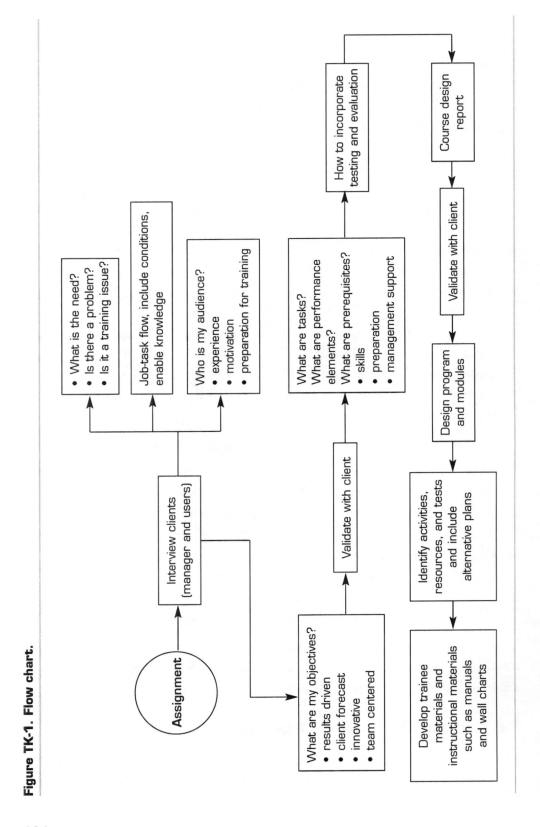

to one another, initial time (perhaps as much as an afternoon or an evening) should be scheduled for them to do their own team building. A much-needed tool is a guide for staff members that not only describes what should be done but also suggests the sequence to be followed.

The staff typically must keep in mind the following considerations as it prepares a training event. Here are 10 easy steps to guide the group through the process:

1. Evaluate the documented training needs.

    ▼ What data do you have on the participants' jobs, home environment, age, gender, and levels of skill?
    ▼ What are the participants' expectations for the training program?
    ▼ Has a proper questionnaire been administered?
    ▼ Has the team seen the program announcement?
    ▼ What is known about the participants' motivation and readiness?
    ▼ What further information does the team need to obtain at the beginning of the program?

2. Set training goals.

    ▼ Discuss and write a set of goals for the program, usually not more than five, and have them ready for use in the first session.
    ▼ Agree among yourselves on the difference between goals and objectives.
    ▼ Be explicit about values, methods, and ground rules.
    ▼ Establish trainer's responsibilities with the design team.

3. Assess staff resources and skills.

    ▼ What training aids have staff members brought with them?
    ▼ What special skills and interests exist among staff members?
    ▼ If certain unusual modules are needed, who can handle them?
    ▼ What resources are required to develop the training response?

4. Select training strategies, and prioritize the order for the program events.

    ▼ This is the heart of the design: What should come first, second, and so forth?
    ▼ Block out the time schedule on a flipchart, and start filling it in.
    ▼ Begin with known elements, such as meals, breaks, and beginning and ending times.
    ▼ As other elements are filled in, look at the schedule's balance, flow, and required energy level.
    ▼ Mornings are better for theory; afternoons are better for activity; evenings are better for nonverbal events.

▼▼▼

One thing should lead to another. Will the experience of the participants be one of growth and development, or will it seem to them that they are getting a series of unconnected inputs?

▲▲▲

5. State the objectives for each module of the program.

  ▼ This may be done by the staff, through discussion, or by the staff members responsible for a specific module.

  ▼ Ideally, the objectives should be specific and measurable: "By the end of this period you should be able to...."

  ▼ Present objectives to participants at the start of each session. Knowing where they are going will help them to learn better.

6. Predict the time schedule for each element of the modules.

  ▼ Each element in the schedule should be specific: introduction, 10 minutes; forming groups and giving instructions, five minutes; working on the task, 40 minutes; and so forth.

  ▼ On a larger scale, make sure that sufficient time is available for what is planned for each training element.

  ▼ Make use of time. Consider how much time the training requires. If you don't have enough time, cover less. The participants will not learn anything if they are hurried through the learning process.

7. Allocate a staff member who will be responsible for each element.

  ▼ Generally, all staff members participate in the first session. Planning this session often takes a large portion of the total planning time. At this meeting, it is best to establish the roles and responsibilities of the members and the expected level of participation. Send a follow-up memo of the discussion and agreement of the roles and responsibilities the next day. Do not wait more than a week. Things change. People forget.

  ▼ For subsequent modules, individual staff members or pairs volunteer to take responsibility.

  ▼ All staff need not participate in planning every session.

  ▼ No one should be overburdened or underused. This is a good time to establish a norm regarding when and how staff members can help one another. For example, they must decide whether it's OK for other staff to interrupt when a staff member is doing a presentation.

▼ ▼ ▼

Schedule time for planning and checking sessions with the staff. Few programs run their course without alteration. When will the staff get together? Can it be done during working hours so that meetings will not consume all available free time or go on late at night?

▲ ▲ ▲

8. Assess the logistical elements.

    ▼ What are the elements of the training location—large room, small room, comfort, convenience?

    ▼ What type of materials are needed—handouts, pencils, flipcharts, name tents, markers, videotapes, reference materials?

    ▼ What are the housekeeping details—breaks, meals, hotels?

    ▼ What administration needs to be completed—registration, money, travel, personal supplies?

    ▼ Is there time for recreation—indoor-outdoor resources, alone time, socializing time?

9. Define the primary clients' concerns.

    ▼ Who is the primary client? Who is paying for the training?

    ▼ What are the client's expectations? How will you communicate?

    ▼ So far, does your design meet the expectations?

    ▼ What contact will you have with the client before, during, and after the program?

    ▼ Will the client be expected to take action as a result of the program?

    ▼ Are you and the client clear on your contract?

10. Provide for an evaluation.

    ▼ Will you evaluate in the following ways as part of the design:
      — by obtaining postmeeting reaction sheets for each module
      — by obtaining a daily rating of satisfaction or learning
      — by obtaining an end-of-program evaluation?

    ▼ Who is going to do the preparation for each of the evaluation methods?

    ▼ Is there any provision for follow-up?

    ▼ Is there a requirement for a report to the primary client?

    ▼ Do you anticipate that the design as planned will meet the goals stated?

Tip 4. Developing Course Objectives

Course objectives should represent a clear statement of what participants should be able to do after they've received the training. This information comes from your task analysis. In practice, therefore, you will have at least twice as many statements as you have tasks on your list. These statements will have the following characteristics:

▼ An objective says something about the learners. It does not describe the resource materials, the trainer, nor the type of learning activity.

▼ An objective describes the learners' behavior or performance. It does not describe the performance of the trainer or what the learners are expected to know or understand. If you use the verb *to understand*, you must go on to explain what learners are expected to do to demonstrate that understanding. Whatever it is you mean by *understanding* would be defined in the sentences to follow the general one.

▼ An objective is about outcomes. It describes an action, not the process the learner went through to get there. The objective describes what the learner is expected to be like at the end of the training, rather than the process the learner used to get to the end.

▼ An objective describes the conditions under which learners will perform the terminal behavior. Remember, anything that the learner will use to perform the task must be defined in the objective statement. For example, a learner will answer three problems with the use of a slide rule or calculator.

▼ An instructional objective also includes information about the level of performance that will be considered acceptable. If a learner will be expected to perform a task within five minutes at the end of a module, this must be stated as part of the objective.

Following are three examples of objectives (Mager 1975):

1. Given an unfinished metal casting, the learner should be able to surface, drill, and tap according to the specifications indicated on the attached blueprint without error in three of five demonstrations.
2. Provided with an outdoor television cable dish kit and appropriate tools, the learner should be able to install the dish and connect the input lead to the telephone line connection. Performance will be judged correct if the dish installation is completed according to trade standards and if the selected cable channels function.
3. Performance: Be able to point out forest fire hazards in a forest area.
   Behavior: Identify dangerous conditions by pointing.

| Conditions: | The learner must have access to forest areas and be exposed to dangerous conditions determined by the instructor. |
| Criteria: | Given a descriptive list of dangerous situations, rank order them according to most to least dangerous. |

Tip 5. Constructing a Course

The most critical part of a training course happens before you enter the training room. Here's an overview of the essential design, development, evaluation, and administration steps. In the design phase, you plan the course. In the development phase, you create the materials and training activities. Evaluation can occur during the analysis, design, development, and implementation phases of instructional development, depending on the type of evaluation. The administration step ties together all of the course elements.

Design

A course design is a guide for developing the training scheme and the learning activities. You develop this scheme on the basis of the learning objectives that you wrote after you conducted the needs assessment.

The course design plan should specify funding categories, such as personnel, equipment and supplies, and facilities. In addition, consider the total budget for the training. Define the scope of the course, and develop a project plan that specifies people's roles and responsibilities and deadlines for course development.

The final equipment and supply list will emerge only after the lesson plans have been completed, but an estimate of the costs should be included.

Objectives

The first step in the course design phase is to determine the training course objective. The course objective states the purpose or benefits of the course; learning objectives state what the learners should know or be able to do after the course; and enabling objectives describe the steps that the learners need to master to achieve the learning objective.

Description

Writing a statement for the course objective is like putting a word puzzle together. Some words you know, others you don't. Here's a list of the information you should include in the description:

▼ why the course is needed, including expected benefits and value of the benefits

- who is involved, including the intended trainees, subject matter experts, supervisors, consultants, and suppliers, as well as their availability for the project
- what the course will cover, including general course content, skill and knowledge areas to be improved, an explanation of how the skill and knowledge areas have been identified and analyzed, and descriptions of how learners will demonstrate the new skill or knowledge
- how the content will be arranged in sequence and what strategies will be used to engage learners in the learning process
- how much the training course is expected to cost and how it will be funded as well as any areas in which cost savings may be realized.

Course and Module Design

During the analysis phase, you identify whether certain tasks are subordinate to others that must be performed in a certain sequence or are unrelated to them. Therefore, you must design the order in which the information will be presented. To maximize the learning, you'll develop a scheme to present this content. Here are a few suggested strategies:

- hierarchical, in which learners receive an overview of the course content before moving to specific elements
- sequential, in which learners are taught steps that lead to a given conclusion
- job order, in which learners are taught tasks as they would occur on the job
- priority order, in which the skill or knowledge areas that are essential to task completion are taught first
- topical order, in which instruction is knowledge based but not sequential, such as the benefits of a new product.

Instructional Strategy

Choose a strategy for each of the learning objectives. The strategy should include the enabling objective and an outline of course content, media, expected feedback mechanism, and level of evaluation and method. The time you invest in planning this stage will ease the development process.

When making decisions about which media are most appropriate to convey the message, assess the costs in a variety of ways to determine which option best suits the investment you're willing to make. Consider, for example:

- whether you'll have to spend a significant amount of money to buy, rent, or purchase a product

- whether you'll have to spend a significant amount of time to locate, create, or develop a product
- whether you'll need assistance from outside the training department, such as from vendors.

Once you've made these decisions, you are ready to move to the development phase.

Development

During the development phase, media and materials will be located, selected, or created. Among the items that need to be gathered, created, or designed are

- instructional guides, such as lesson plans, bridges that lead from one instructional activity to the next
- integrators that serve to tie activities together and align them with the learner's prior learning
- administrative aids, such as participant rosters, maps, checklists for materials and equipment, and name tags for learners
- learner guides, such as text, workbooks, and job aids
- evaluation materials
- activity aids, such as checklists, role-play scripts, case studies, and laboratory exercises
- equipment and supplies, paper, videotapes, VCRs, films, wall charts, computers, flipcharts, markers, and spare equipment parts.

Evaluation

An evaluation may be formative or summative, but it must be tied to the course and the learning objectives. A formative evaluation continues throughout the analysis, design, development, and implementation phases of instructional development. A formative evaluation plan describes the means for improving a course and assessing learners' training progress and attitudes toward the training. A summative evaluation occurs after course completion. A summative evaluation plan describes such measures as posttraining performance, turnover, and customer comments.

By answering questions about tasks, topics, learning activities, materials, tests, and productivity, evaluations can lead to course refinements. Evaluations can be conducted at the objectives level through tests of learners' mastery of the enabling objectives or the learning objectives. Evaluations also may be conducted by using group-related and enabling objectives. The trainer executes this method by asking each group of learners to write one question on any topic or issue that they feel needs to be clarified. The trainer can either answer questions posed by each group or rotate each set of questions and have each group of learners answer a neighboring group's question. After completing this step, the trainer should take note of anything that seems to be a design course or material development issue and share it with the course designer. It could be that material needs to be added or deleted to ensure that the evaluation adequately tests the learners against the standards for the targeted objective.

Administration

Course administration ties together all of the course elements—the enabling, learning, and course objectives. This is the last step before the course presentation. At this stage you add bridges, special learning activities, and variety.

Among the items to be considered are the following:

- ▼ **Activity sequence**: What were the learners doing immediately before the presentation of the objective? What will they be doing immediately after? What relationship exists between the previous and subsequent activities? Are the learners aware of the relationship? Is there a logical transition from one activity to the next?

- ▼ **Directions**: What instructions will the trainer need to convey the information or content? How specific should they be? What instructions do the learners need to complete any participatory activities? How will tests be conducted?

- ▼ **Materials**: What visual aids or handouts are needed? Are they in order and ready when required? Are all supplies available? Are props such as models or reference books handy?

- ▼ **Hardware**: What kind of equipment—models, videotape players, flipcharts, computers—is required by the content? Are they in good working order? Are spare parts or alternative methods available in the event of equipment failure?

- ▼ **Special environments**: If a training program requires a special environment, like a computer lab, is that environment available?

- ▼ **Class management**: What are the requirements for conducting the course, for example, the optimal number of learners? What seating arrangements are required? Is special access needed for any handicapped learners? Will lunch or coffee be served? How will this service be handled?

- ▼ **Required records**: The course design document will detail what course records will be kept, how, by whom, and for how long. Training records may be kept on paper, computer disks, or CDs. Original or back-up records may be maintained in the training information system or the planning or legal departments.

▼ **Standards of performance**: Training designs should be performance based, that is, the training should focus on mastery of skills that can be immediately transferred back on the job.

Original training records or copies may need to be forwarded to a government agency, private regulatory group, or professional agency that issues credentials. Record retention and destruction schedules may be established by law, organizational policies, or the design team's recommendation.

During development, any documentation materials could be copied. For example, the training department probably has a standard, daily attendance form that needs only to be copied. But a new legally mandated course might require a form that documents employees' attendance in specific units of a course.

An organization will typically keep a history that shows responsibility for various aspects of course development; form samples, course design document, and lesson plans; budgets; attendance by learners, trainers, facilitators, and guests; and evaluation records about individual participants, instructor's performance, and course effectiveness or efficiency.

The standards of successful job performance must be clear to the learners by the trainers, and success in training should be measured by the successful transfer of learning. Successful training programs are designed around what the learners need to know and how to transfer the learning into on-the-job performance.

Tip 6. Dealing With Difficult Situations

Every training session is different, and every learner is different. Following is a list of the most frequently occurring difficult situations along with suggested ways to resolve them.

▼ **The group remains silent**. There are times when groups are silent, and that's fine. Other times, when groups should be interactive and engaging, they look at you with dead stares and keep silent. This is a scary situation for the trainer. One of the things that you can do is check it out. Ask the group if there is a reason for their silence. It could be that they don't understand what you are presenting, that your method of delivery is one they're not familiar with.

▼ **Things are moving too quickly**. Sometimes the group picks up something that you have said that relates to material that you'll cover later. You can respond simply and state when you are going to cover it, or if shifting the piece of information or module makes sense, you can insert it during the present discussion. Not all learners are comfortable with taking things out of the design sequence, however, so you might request a show of hands on whether to change the order.

▼ **Things are moving too slowly**. The group may not be motivated to listen to your topic, or the group may have expected you to present something other than what you are presenting. If this occurs during training, try to build on things the participants already know if it seems to you that the information is too basic; don't speed up your presentation, but encourage trainees to participate. Situations like this are good times to develop an in-class game, conduct a competitive team answer quiz, or find another way to enliven the lesson.

▼ **A talkative learner is in the group**. This is fine unless the person dominates every conversation. One suggestion is that you enlist that person's help as an expert. Another idea is to talk with the person during the break, acknowledging expertise and suggesting you work together so everyone has an opportunity to participate.

▼ **A silent learner, one who does not ask questions, is in the group**. Don't jump to conclusions about silent learners. Although it appears that they're not listening or participating, they might be auditory learners, who listen, process, and only ask questions or make comments when it is essential for clarifying something that is confusing. If one is in the group, first check out the person's learning style. If you find the situation is not one of learning style, try to bring the person into the group. Assign the person to a caring participant or group. Tread cautiously. Start with asking fairly easy questions or ask the person to share an experience. If all else fails, during the break you might ask the person in a private conversation how the training is going. Find out if there is anything that the person might need.

▼ **A typical know-it-all is in the group**. The know-it-all corrects everyone constantly, sometimes you. Don't kill the person on sight. Find out what's going on. Or as happens in most group situations, the group will sort this problem out for you.

▼ **A session is getting sidetracked**. Sometimes a conversation starts in the right direction but finishes up in the wrong place. Acknowledge this, and get the group back on track. You might want to have a person in the group monitor those side trips. Have someone in each group be a parking lot attendant by recording issues that need attention and placing them in the parking lot until you can address them.

▼ **The trainer and a learner have personality problems.** Occasionally you'll have a personality clash with one of the participants. The professional trainer must ignore this and continue treating that participant in a normal manner. Avoid letting the group see the problem.

▼ **Participants have personality problems.** Personality problems do occur in the classroom environment because people don't leave their personalities at the door. If arguments start between participants, cut in quickly. Ask others for comments on the issue. Try to keep the personalities separated. If the situation is not resolved, during the break, have a frank discussion with both parties.

▼ **A rambler is in the group.** Some people learn by speaking. A rambling participant could be this person. Practice good active listening techniques. Ask the rambler for the bottom-line message so that the whole group might participate. Be patient. Be polite yet firm in bringing the discussion to a close.

▼ **An arguer is in the group.** This person might also have to be put in the trainer's blind spot. Most of the time, the group will take care of this type. Use your judgment. You could suggest that the discussion continue after class or that the class devote some time for the specific issue during a lunch discussion.

▼ **A complainer is in the group.** If the complaint is not something that must be addressed, you could explore the issue briefly, but don't waste the group's time on it. If you get complaints about the organization, let the participants know this is not the correct forum to discuss a change in policy.

▼ **Side conversation takes place during training.** Although I've seen some trainers ask people who talk during training to share their conversation, I don't suggest this at all. Instead, change their seats or talk to the people. But don't gang up on them. In this kind of situation, the group will always support the learners, no matter how badly they've behaved. Polite, non-threatening action is the way to handle this situation.

▼ **A learner gives a definitely wrong response.** Don't embarrass the person by saying the answer is wrong. Acknowledge the person's point of view, and suggest considering some additional data. Or you could use the correct information in a summary of the person's response. Some trainers suggest asking the participants for their comments, but be careful with this strategy. Participants may embarrass one another or become contentious, and you may not have the power to resolve the dispute.

Tip 7. Training Types

An easy way to design a training event is to use a template. Over the years, I have observed that there exists a dynamic in training and learning. Basically, the training event process occurs when the trainer drives the learning event, meaning that each step of the event is controlled by the trainer. The other template you can use to develop training is to have the material drive the learning process; the sequence of the learning event is dictated by the way the topic is organized and sequenced for training delivery.

Training Formats

There are two types of training strategies: learner-centered and trainer-centered. In learner-centered training, learners control the learning process. They set the pace and the amount of material to be covered. In learner-centered training, the trainer and learner typically have two-way communication and a collaborative dialogue. Distance learning courses are learner centered.

In trainer-centered learning, the trainer establishes the format, the content, and the timing. Lectures are trainer centered. Communication is one way, and the trainer controls the dialogue.

The most common training formats are as follows:

- **Classroom**: This is a traditional approach to training. In most cases, this is structured seating, usually in rows, a given agenda, and little active movement. The classroom style is conducive to lectures.

- **Outdoor adventures**: This learner-centered format is sometimes referred to as an adventure learning event. The military has used this format. This method has been used for building team training and leadership development. To be effective, it must be linked to meaningful classroom input and an extensive debriefing session. Also, make sure you look into the insurance liability issue before you decide to develop your program using this method.

- **Computer assisted**: Sometimes called computer-based training or programmed learning, this learner-centered method teaches people material at computer workstations in a programmed way; the lessons in the programmed learning are usually designed and developed as action-based tasks, or in other words, step-by-step. With the spread of computers and telecourses, this process provides flexibility so that learners can control their pace. The disadvantage is that learners are most often alone during the learning sessions. If you are thinking about using this method, conduct a thorough cost analysis to determine the need and the magnitude of the use and stability of the information (avoid constant updates) before making the investment.

▼ **Training media:** These media include overhead projectors, flipcharts and PowerPoint presentations, which are used in trainer-centered formats; videotapes and LCDs can be used in either learner- or trainer-centered formats. When using instructional media, aim for a variety in both method and media to break up the learners' experience and enable the training message to get through on different levels.

Training Roles

Trainers have to wear different hats. In some companies, a trainer will be able to share responsibilities with other people in the training department, but in other companies one person may have several roles. A subject matter expert will be able to assist a trainer in areas where the trainer does not have expertise.

▼ **Trainer:** The role of the trainer is to facilitate learning so that learners can acquire the key competencies presented. A trainer should be good at presenting information so that the attention of the audience is held and the information is accurately conveyed.

▼ **Method expert:** As a trainer, you must exercise sound, professional judgment about the best process in presenting and facilitating learning. Becoming competent with a variety of learning techniques should be your constant goal and part of your professional development plan. Watch other trainers, attend training events, read about training, and share ideas with other trainers. Take risks by trying different training methods and experimenting.

▼ **Group manager:** The role of the group manager takes a while to acquire. Subject competency can be acquired fairly quickly, but group facilitation skills take much longer. A good, experienced facilitator has a skill of enormous power and is able to harness the synergy within the group to achieve powerful and lasting learning. It is a competency you should strive to acquire, and it is best acquired through practice.

▼ **Subject matter expert:** The subject mater expert knows the content and task well and is responsible for providing information about them. Whereas the trainer is responsible for designing and developing the content and process so that trainees comprehend and use the information provided, the subject mater expert is the quality control person who ensures the accuracy of the training. The subject mater expert is your partner in designing and delivering training.

Tip 8. Creating Games, Simulations, and Role Plays

Through games, simulations, and role plays, learners can discover learning outcomes on their own, without being told everything. The ultimate outcome for using games, simulations, and role plays is to improve learning.

▼ **Games:** A game is an activity, illustration, or exercise that can support the point the trainer presents. Typically, games are brief, nonthreatening learning events in which all learners participate. They should have simple, uncomplicated directions and a stated purpose that are consistent with the key competencies being taught, and, in most cases, they should be fun.

▼ **Simulations:** Sometimes referred to as case studies in action, simulations are highly participative, used mainly to teach skills, and linked to real-world situations. Simulations can be simple paper mock-ups or an exact replica of something like a tractor or nuclear reactor. Flight simulations in which pilots learn flying skills and procedures for dealing with emergency situations, for example, are realistic imitations of the real world. Another example is an in-box exercise for manager or office producers in which an entire office process is replicated with assigned roles, dialogues, and feedback mechanisms.

▼ **Role plays:** A role play is similar to a simulation. Normally the only prop needed for the role play is a script or short case study or problem, which the learners will act out. The problem is usually related to a situation at work that involves the players. After the role players have identified the problem, they act out the parts either as they would normally or by trying new behaviors. Following the role play, the players, often as well as other group members, provide feedback by identifying good and bad points, suggesting other forms of behavior, and recommending other alternatives. In a training situation, use this method of instruction selectively. Carefully judge the appropriate time for it because learners get bored with the format. Vary it by using other peripherals or methods.

Tip 9. Using Individualized Instruction

Successful individualized instruction requires the completion of four major phases. Each phase is equally important and should be completed in sequence to ensure that you obtain the expected results from the training event. Omission of any of these phases can seriously affect the effectiveness of the tutorial program. Following are descriptions of each of the four phases:

1. **Preparation**: Ask the learners to define the problem or areas of need; have them do the necessary analysis to ensure that there is a focused training need. Take the defined needs and develop a list of targeted training topics. Check this list with the learners. Once you have a list of targeted topics, ask the learners to do a job breakdown. Learners must identify with their specific needs for training before they can comprehend the why's and what's of their job. You can use the job breakdown to establish the design of your training course and cluster your proposed training topics.

2. **Presentation**: Once you have provided the initial rationale as to why the topics are sequenced and how each piece of information you are to present is aligned, you are ready to begin the tutorial. The tutorial consists of the following three steps:

   Step 1: Show and tell how it is done.

   Step 2: Demonstrate while asking the learner to explain why it's being done the way it is.

   Step 3: Tell the learner what to do, and have the learners do each step while explaining how and why it should be done that way. If at any point the learners provide incorrect information while explaining, coach them until they have the correct information.

3. **Performance**: Learners try to perform each step of the assigned task. The performance phase is frequently repeated several times so that the learners have a chance to check for understanding. One way to accomplish this task is to ask the learners to explain what they are going to do, how they will do it, and why. Here you are checking to determine if the learners mastered the concepts. Check for understanding of both the content and the process. It may appear that the learners have mastered the content concepts but interpreted the process differently. If the difference is a result of the learning styles, there is no problem. If the process is muddled, however, it usually means that the learners have muddled the process conceptually and not learned the parts well. By using this repetition in both the presentation and performance phases of the training sequence, the learner goes through the process at least five times. By this time, the learners have the key learning points mastered.

4. **Follow-up**: The follow-up phase can be crucial to maintaining the mastery of the newly learned concepts. Once the learners perform adequately, check occasionally to make sure they are using the proper methods. This step is going to be difficult for you to administer unless you give the learners a post-tutorial assignment and reach some agreement prior to departure as to how you both are going to manage this process.

Preparing for Tutorial Instruction

To prepare to conduct a tutorial, you have to know both the nature of the training need and the nature of the skills or knowledge that you'll be presenting to the learners. So in this first step, you'll have to collect and review all the necessary data and organize it. Use the self-preparation checklist to help you:

▼ Describe and define the nature of the training situation.

▼ Analyze the situation, and make sure that tutorial training is appropriate.

▼ Review the worksheets that you used to map out your training proposal. Make sure that you state a theoretical concept in your proposed design and development strategy.

▼ Prepare training objectives for the training. Decide where you're going and what you plan to accomplish in the training event.

▼ Prepare a job task breakdown sheet for each task that will be taught.

▼ Prepare a learning outline.

▼ Schedule an appropriate time and place for the training.

▼ Assemble any training aids or materials that you will need for the training. Assemble all materials and supplies, set up the equipment, and make other final preparations for the training.

When you've gotten yourself ready and the materials and the training site set up, and the learners have shown up for the tutorial, it's time to prepare the learners.

Preparing the Learners

Trainers often overlook this step, but it is very important in getting the learners in the right frame of mind to enter the training process. This is where you, the trainer, begin to apply the ARAB effectiveness key:

A = Arouse
R = Reward
A = Assess
B = Build.

You *arouse* the learners' curiosity and obtain an interest in the training; you *build* or maintain the learners' motivation. And although *reward* and reinforcement will probably have to wait until the learners actually try out the newly learned concepts back on the job, you still *assess* the learning transfer before they go back in the workplace and make the appropriate learning links for the learners before they leave.

Presenting the Training

Now that you're ready to do the training, and the learners have been motivated to view the coming training in a favorable light, you're ready to explain the actual steps of the tutorial. This could be referred to as the show-and-tell step of the training. You'll be showing the steps of the course, telling how to perform them, and explaining why the training (and the related job) is done the way it is.

Tip 10. Developing Contract Learning

Contract learning is a form of self-directed learning. Contract learning lets learners decide the topics or competencies they want to learn and how they want to learn them. Each learner can devise the topics to be mastered or the issues to be researched. This type of learning has a lot of advantages over the classroom style in which learners may just sit and listen to a lecture or become minimally involved.

In contract learning, trainers and learners prepare the contract. Learners also have the opportunity to write their own objectives and determine what work is going to be done, what resources are going to be used, and how to design the evaluation criteria. Because learners write so much, they really own the project. This sense of ownership gives them the motivation to carry the contract through to the finish.

Learning Contract

The learning contact is a written agreement between the learners and the trainer. In it, the learners and the trainer establish that one or more competencies need to be raised to a higher level of expertise. Given this need statement, the learners enter into a formal, written agreement with the trainer.

Once the two parties agree on the basic learning competencies, the learners and the trainer must agree on the learning objectives, resources, proof of goals met, and evaluation process. Contract learning may be fully a learner-based process that the learners conduct without a trainer. That approach might be problematic because no one would be able to check the administration of the training and keep the learners on track. If the learners were unable to establish a workable contract, they could become discouraged and sidetracked from learning.

The typical contract has nine steps, as figure TK-2 shows. Through their negotiations, however, learners and trainers may choose more or fewer steps as they reach acceptable terms. The key points for learners are that the contract contains a structure, objective, evaluation method, and targeted learning outcomes.

Figure TK-2. Nine stages of a contract.

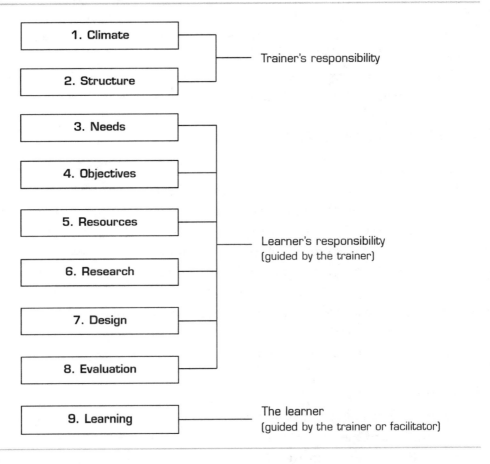

Contract Elements

A number of styles are possible for learner contracts, but the most popular is a letter format. The elements for the letter come from a form like that in figure TK-3.

Before the learners and the trainer can formulate a contract, they must identify the level of competency. Then they can develop one or more specific learning objectives. These statements must define what the learner will learn, not what that person will be doing.

Then the learners must establish the process for monitoring the contract, the resources needed, and the learning strategies required for meeting the objectives. These could include meeting or speaking with a subject matter expert; watching videotapes; reading specific literature; or working in a specific situation, whether real or simulated.

Next, the learners must define what will be evaluated. This section of the contract should contain specific statements as to products or actions that provide evidence of mastery. Examples might include essays, reports, projects, problem-solving situations, videotaped presentations, rating scales, or anything else that the evaluator can use to establish evidence of task accomplishment.

In the fourth section, the learners provide the measurement criteria. The learners could specify the length of an end-of-project report, standards for videotapes, required content and format for reports and the review process, criteria for evaluations, and comments or feedback.

Figure TK-3. Elements of a learning contract.

Student: _____ Competency: _____
Date Commenced:___/___/___
Trainer:_____ Date Due: ___/___/___

1. Learning objectives	2. Resource strategies	3. What is to be assessed?	4. How is it to be assessed?
Write all of the learning objectives here. The learners should design more than one objective. The objectives must be easy to understand and describe the learning, not the doing.	List all resources and strategies here. Include not only books and films but also human resources. There also may be a number of other items that need to be carried out by the learner; they should be included here.	The things that are being assessed should relate directly to the stated learning objectives. However, here we are normally looking at what has been done. This could include reports, essays, videotapes, diary details, or situations.	Assessment could state the length of the report or essay. It could include a timeframe for a video presentation. It also could state that certain experts must agree with the results and the process by which they were achieved. Did the trainer think the resources were used effectively?

(Please note that these are only suggestions. Anything can be included as long as both the learners and the trainer agree to its relevance and appropriateness.)

Approved: Yes ☐ Advisor's signature:_____

  No ☐

Date: ___/___/___ Learner's signature: _____

When the learners have completed these four elements, both parties will review the contract and then sign it. But before the parties sign the contract, they should make sure the contract is a sound document:

- ▼ Are the learning objectives specific?
- ▼ Do the objectives relate to the learning task?
- ▼ Are the resources and strategies appropriate to achieve the outcome?
- ▼ Can the learners think of any other forms of evaluation?
- ▼ Are the evaluation criteria fair?
- ▼ Has the evaluation process been established?
- ▼ Have the steps for completing and presenting the contract learning been defined?

Contractual Learning

Contract learning can be developed for any learning situation; it is a learning process. It can be of value to both learners and trainers because there are benefits to both in managing the process. The benefit for the trainer in this process is facilitating the learning process and helping learners achieve their goals.

In designing this self-directed learning process, the trainer must create a process that involves learners' participation from the initial stage. This involvement serves two purposes. One, it sets the scene for learners to design what they want to learn, the format for the learning, and the outcome, and two, it allows learners to take maximum responsibility for the learning process.

Learning contracts help to solve problems associated with the differences in educational backgrounds, life experiences, personal interests, job experiences, different forms of motivation, and general abilities of the individuals.

Tip 11. Ensuring Retention

To ensure learners retain what they've learned, consider designing one or more review techniques. Listed below are several recommended techniques:

- ▼ Identify what the learners have learned, not what the trainer has trained. Tests are a judge only of what the trainer has provided. They don't measure what's important to the learners.
- ▼ For maximum retention, vary the ways to learn what you are training and review the content at least six times during the training day.

▼ Involve the learners. People remember things that are different, colorful, and graphic.

▼ Create handouts so trainees have something concrete to take with them when they leave. These are far more effective than oral summaries.

Technique 1. What Did You Learn?
What You Need
▼ Six blank flipchart sheets
▼ Markers.

How to Do It
▼ Each person visits each sheet twice to record a learning point from the training.
▼ Each point is different (no repeats).
▼ Divide large groups into small groups, and have them update the lists.
▼ Check any item a learner does not understand. The person who writes it must explain it.

Technique 2. One Blooming Point!
What You Need
▼ An inflated, different-colored balloon for each table
▼ Small sticky notes.

How to Do It
▼ Each balloon has a label relevant to a topic covered.
▼ Each member of the table writes one idea about the topic on a sticky note and attaches it to the balloon.
▼ The balloon with the sticky notes remains at the table for the duration of the session. As participants remember ideas, they can add additional sticky notes.

Technique 3. Collect the Dots
What You Need
▼ Colored dots
▼ Markers
▼ Flipchart sheets—one for each table or group; each sheet should list specific topics under discussion.

How to Do It

- ▽ Each morning, provide colored dots. Each person gets a different colored dot.
- ▽ Each person marks with a dot anything useful or relevant to work that is on the flipchart.
- ▽ At day's end, participants identify their dots on the flipchart sheet.

Technique 4. Three Important Things

What You Need

- ▽ Flipchart sheets
- ▽ Markers.

How to Do It

- ▽ Give this take-away assignment at the day's end: identify three things you learned today.
- ▽ The next morning, each participant will list the three on a flipchart.
- ▽ Keep each sheet posted on a wall.

Technique 5. Surprise Catch

What You Need

- ▽ Ball.

How to Do It

- ▽ Participants stand. Instructor models behavior: "I choose [name of a participant]," and throws the ball. The person who catches the ball must call out a learning point from the day before.
- ▽ The catcher then becomes the pitcher and throws the ball to another participant. Once the ball is tossed, that pitcher sits down.

Technique 6. True-or-False Questions

What You Need

- ▽ 3″ × 5″ cards.

How to Do It

- ▽ Have each group construct true-or-false questions based on the previous day's learning.
- ▽ Teams compete answering them. When a team answers incorrectly, it sits down. The last team standing wins.

Technique 7. Jeopardy

What You Need

▼ 3″ × 5″ cards.

How to Do It

▼ Have each table write content questions, one to a card. Collect them.

▼ Line up the entire group, dividing them into two groups against two walls, spelling bee fashion.

▼ Rotate asking questions to the first person in line on one side, and then on the other side. If the answer is wrong, the person sits down.

▼ Continue until one team eliminates the other.

Technique 8. Concept Puzzles

What You Need

▼ Colored cardboard (six to eight colors).

How to Do It

▼ Cut out simple puzzle pieces from each sheet of cardboard, and list one concept per puzzle piece.

▼ Have each person take a piece of a puzzle.

▼ Put the people holding all like-colored pieces together at the same table.

▼ The group puts the puzzle together and lists six to eight learning points about the topics on each puzzle piece.

Technique 9. Card Game

What You Need

▼ 3″ × 5″ cards.

How to Do It

▼ Give one card to each participant, and have each participant write one question about the content.

▼ Collect the cards, shuffle, and deal equally to each table.

▼ Give the participants 15 minutes to answer the questions, using all resources available.

▼ Have the participants list the answers on a flipchart.

▼ Review the questions as a group.

Technique 10. The Most Useful

What You Need

- ▼ Sticky dots
- ▼ Flipchart sheets
- ▼ Markers.

How to Do It

- ▼ Headline each sheet "The Most Useful Thing I Learned [date of last session]."
- ▼ Each table lists the most useful things it comes up with, leaving space between statements.
- ▼ Other participants move among the charts, dotting with their initials each statement, and trying to piggyback an idea onto each statement. (Make sure that each participant lists a related idea under each statement initialed.)

Technique 11. Correct the Errors

What You Need

- ▼ Overhead projector
- ▼ Transparencies
- ▼ Green pens.

How to Do It

- ▼ Create transparencies with content errors.
- ▼ Each participant should discover what the error is, write it down, and provide the correct answer.
- ▼ Each group compares the list of errors and corrections.
- ▼ Debrief the entire group.

Technique 12. Developing a Picture

What You Need

- ▼ Flipchart sheets
- ▼ Markers.

How to Do It

- ▼ Assign each table a portion of a topic.
- ▼ Tell the participants that there will be a visitor who knows nothing about the topic.

▼ Each table is to present the highlights of the topic.

▼ Invite one or two guests to listen to the presentations. Ideally, guests should be stakeholders in the training.

Tip 12. Demonstrating a Skill

A skill is a set of steps. Some examples of skills include word processing, driving, scuba diving, and flying a plane. Some skills require simple actions; other skills are more complex.

All skills require the use of three types of skills: motor, perceptual, and cognitive. A demonstration, generally, requires a combination of the skill types. This combination of motor, perceptual, and cognitive skills is given the term *psychomotor* skill. Therefore, regardless of the type of skill that you may be demonstrating, you must be mindful that all three skill areas are involved in the process. The demonstration process consists of four sections: preparation, demonstration, practice, and assessment.

Preparation

The following steps in the process are an overview of the steps to help you prepare for the training event:

▼ Establish the current level of trainee knowledge or ability in the area to be presented.

▼ Discuss the skill to be presented with other subject matter experts, analyze the skill, and break it down into manageable, teachable parts.

▼ Draft a plan for conducting the demonstration.

▼ Prepare the support materials for the training event: job aids, wall charts, videotapes, and so forth.

▼ Prepare lesson objectives and test items.

▼ Prepare an introduction to the training event that is appropriate to the situation.

Demonstration

It's important that you do the demonstration correctly—no flaws because you're modeling. There are a number of suggested ways to present a demonstration. The following method has seven steps.

1. **Demonstrate at normal speed**: Demonstrate the skill correctly, at normal speed, so that trainees can see the final results and also see what is expected from them at the conclusion of the training.

2. **Demonstrate again slowly**: Demonstrate again for the trainees, this time doing it slowly so they can see exactly what is being done. As the trainer demonstrates, trainees should begin to recognize names, parts, tools, and obvious skills. When demonstrating and explaining how the skill is performed, trainers must be careful about what they say and how they say it. The trainer should introduce each step, then highlight the key points with deliberate and possibly exaggerated movements. These key points also can be highlighted by voice, by giving reasons, or perhaps by repetition. It's a good idea to pause between key points to let them sink in. The demonstrator must have a set of notes or a skills sheet to follow for this part of the demonstration. The skills sheet gives a complete breakdown of the skills, with the key points highlighted, and any tricks of the trade and safety points noted, as figure TK-4 shows.

3. **Verbal instruction from the trainees**: Get the trainees to tell you how to carry out the task in the correct sequence. The demonstrator carries out the performance as instructed by the trainees.

Figure TK-4. Sample skill sheet.

Operations	Key Points	Safety
Assemble Position tank	• Stand tank up • O-ring facing away	• Don't leave tank standing unattended
Position BCD	• Slide over tank • BCD facing away • Height of BCD should be half way up tank valve • Adjust to fit different size tanks (63 and 88) • Lock in position	• Avoid hitting head on tank valve • Must be secure so it doesn't fall out when straps are set
Position and attach regulator	• Remove dust cap • Regulator and octopus to right side • Machined face to O-ring • Do up finger tight • Connect low pressure inflator to DCD	• Keep out sand • Check O-ring is there • If too tight cannot undo later • Pull knurled nut back

Operations	Key Points	Safety
Turn on air	• Turn tank on	• Slowly check position of gauges On and back half turn What to do if O-ring missing
	• Check tank pressure	• Must be full to commence dive
	• Check second stage regulator • Check octopus	• Must breath easily
	• Check L.P. inflator	• Must inflate and deflate
Lay down	• Gauges and regulators in front	• Keep out sand and grass
Dismantle To turn off	• Turn air off • Purge lines	• Not over tight
Remove regulator	• Disconnect L.P. inflator • Undo nut • Replace dust cap • Place regulator away	• Must be dry
Remove BCD	• Undo Velcro • Slide off tank • Place BCD away	• Hold tank
Tank	• Lay tank down	• So it won't fall
Final Rinse all equipment		• Don't push purge button

Practice

4. **Controlled trainee performance:** Have the trainees carry out the skills under close supervision and at a controlled pace. It is important that the trainees perform this correctly. It is difficult, and sometimes impossible, to counteract the effects of skills learned incorrectly.

5. **Student practice:** Now is the time for students to practice. This part of a skills session should be at least 50 percent of the allocated session time. During this time, the demonstrator must be available to answer any questions that arise. Don't take over for trainees who have problems, but have them correct the

problem themselves. The trainer or other members of the group can provide the correct information or suggestions. Try to enlist their peers to assist with any problems.

Assessment

6. **Student assessment:** Some form of assessment must take place to ensure that the trainees have reached the stated objectives and standards that were described at the beginning of the session. Assessment may be done during the session by asking questions, or it may be done at the end of the session by using some form of test. The type of assessment depends on the demonstrator and the type of skills being instructed. An important point with assessment is that trainees should be expecting the type of test you give. The test also must be appropriate to the topic and the learning event.

7. **Conclusion:** The session must conclude with the demonstrator summarizing the main points of the session and clarifying any areas of concern. If possible, all test results should be made available before the end of the session, so they might be included in the conclusion.

References

Chapter 1

Aldrich, C. "Global learning, 2008." *The AMA Handbook of E-Learning: Effective Design, Implementation, and Technology Solutions*, G. M. Piskurich, editor. New York: AMACOM, 2003.

Balaguer, E. "Facing the future: 5 questions." *T+D*, volume 60, number 1, 2006.

Bennis, W., W. W. Burke, G. Gery, W. M. Juechter, G. Rummler, and N. Tichy. "What lies ahead." *T+D*, volume 57, number 1, 2003.

Bunker, K. A. "When a classroom revolt is a good thing." *T+D*, volume 60, number 1, 2006.

Cole, S., S. Gale, S. Greengard, P. Kieger, C. Lachnitt, T. Raphael, D. Shiut, and J. Wiscombe. "Fast forward: 25 trends that will change the way you do business." *Workforce*, volume 82, number 6, June 2003.

Davenport, R. F. "Future of the profession." *T+D*, volume 60, number 1, January 2006.

McArdle, G. *Training Design & Development*. Alexandria, VA: ASTD Press, 1999.

McLagan, P., and R. McCullough. *Models for excellence: The conclusions and recommendations of the ASTD training and development competency study*. Alexandria, VA: ASTD, 1989.

Rothwell, W. J., and H. J. Sredl. *The ASTD Reference Guide to Workplace Learning and Performance: Present and Future Roles and Competencies* (3rd edition). Amherst, MA: Human Resource Development Press, 2000.

Sugrue, B., and R. Rivera. *2005 State of the Industry Report*. Alexandria, VA: ASTD Press, 2005.

Thompson, C., E. Koon, W. H. Woodwell Jr., and J. Beauvais. *Training for the Next Economy: An ASTD State of the Industry Report on Trends in Employer-Provided Training in the United States*. Alexandria, VA: ASTD, 2002.

Chapter 2

Bernthal, P. R., K. Colteryahn, P. Davis, J. Naughton, W. J. Rothwell, and R. Wellins. *ASTD Competency Study: Mapping the Future.* Alexandria, VA: ASTD, 2004.

Fitz-enz, J. *The ROI of Human Capital: Measuring the Economic Value of Employee Performance.* New York: AMACOM, 2000.

Furjanic, S. W., and L. A. Trotman. *Turning Training Into Learning: How to Design and Deliver Programs that Get Results.* New York: AMACOM, 2000.

Harris, P. "Outsourced Learning: A New Market." *T+D*, volume 57, number 9, 2003.

Jackson, T. "The Management of People Across Cultures: Valuing People Differently." *Human Resource Management*, volume 41, number 4, 2002.

Kirkpatrick, D. L. "Techniques for evaluating training programs." *Training and Development Journal*, volume 33, number 6, 1979.

McArdle, G. "The AMA Trainers' Activity Book." *Problem-Based Learning: A New Teaching Tool.* New York: AMACOM, 2004.

Perkins, D. *Outsmarting IQ: The Emerging Science of Learnable Intelligence.* New York: The Free Press, 1995.

Rose, C., and M. J. Nicholl. *Accelerated Learning for the 21st Century: The Six-Step Plan to Unlock Your Master-Mind.* New York: Dell Publishing, 1998.

Russo, C. *The Early Bird Guide to ASTD Professional Certification: Your Jump Start to CPLP Certification.* Alexandria, VA: ASTD, 2005.

Spitzer, D. R. "The Design and Development of High Impact Interventions." *Handbook of Human Performance Technology*, H. D. Stolovich and E. Keeps, editors. San Francisco: Jossey-Bass, 2000.

Swanson, R. A., and E. F. Holton. *Results: How to Access Performance, Learning, and Perceptions in Organizations.* San Francisco: Berrett-Koehler Publishers, 1999.

Vygotsky, L. S. *Mind in Society: The Development of Higher Psychological Processes.* Cambridge, MA: Harvard University Press, 1978.

Walter, K. "Bring on the Entertainment." *Personnel Journal*, July 1995.

Chapter 3

Blanchard, P. N., and J. C. Thacker. *Effective Training: Systems, Strategies, and Practices* (2nd edition). New Jersey: Pearson Education, 2004.

Brannick, M. T., and E. L. Levine. *Job Analysis: Methods, Research, and Applications for Human Resource Management in the New Millennium.* Thousand Oaks, CA: Sage Publication, 2002.

Filipczak, B. "Different Strokes: Learning Styles in the Classroom," *Training*, March 1995. Available at www.trainingmag.com.

Kaye, B., and B. Jacobson. "True Tales and Tall Tales: The Power of Organizational Story Telling." *Training and Development*, March 1999.

Lacey, K. "Building Bridges—Making Mentoring Happen." *Training and Development in Australia*, October 1999.

Lawson, K. *Improving On-the-Job Training and Coaching.* Alexandria: VA: ASTD, 1997.

Marquardt, M. *Action Learning in Action: Transforming Problems and People for World-Class Organizational Learning.* Palo Alto, CA: Davies-Black Publishing, 1999.

McArdle, G. *Training Design & Development.* Alexandria, VA: ASTD Press, 1999.

Rothwell, W. J., editor. *ASTD Models for Human Performance Improvement: Roles, Competencies, and Outputs.* Alexandria: VA: ASTD, 1998.

Rothwell, W. J., and H. C. Kazanas. *Mastering the Instructional Design Process: A Systematic Approach* (2nd edition). San Francisco: Jossey-Bass, 1998.

Rylatt, A. *Learning Unlimited, Practical Strategies for Transforming Learning in the Workplace of the 21st Century* (2nd edition). NSW Australia: Business + Publishing, 2000.

Chapter 4

Cooper, K. C. *Effective Competency Modeling and Reporting: A Step-by-Step Guide for Improving Individual and Organizational Performance.* New York: AMACOM, 2000.

Draves, W. A. *Energizing the Learning Environment.* New York: Learning Resources Network, 1995.

Dubois, D. D., and W. J. Rothwell. *The Competency Toolkit* (volume 1). Amherst, MA: Human Resource Development Press, 2000.

———. *Competency-Based Human Resource Management.* Palo Alto, CA: Davies-Black Publishing, 2004.

Eiffert, S. D. *Cross-Train Your Brain: A Mental Fitness Program for Maximizing Creativity and Achieving Success.* New York: AMACOM, 1999.

Lucas, R. *The Creative Training Idea Book: Inspired Tips and Techniques for Engaging and Effective Learning.* New York: AMACOM, 2003.

Meier, D. *The Accelerated Learning Handbook: A Creative Guide to Designing and Delivering Faster, More Creative Training Programs.* New York: McGraw-Hill, 2000.

Rossett, A. *The ASTD E-Learning Handbook: Best Practices, Strategies, and Cases Studies for an Emerging Field.* New York: McGraw-Hill, 2001.

Van Buren, M. E., and W. Erskine. *State of the Industry: ASTD's Annual Review of Trends in Employer-Provided Training in the United States.* Alexandria, VA: ASTD, 2002.

Chapter 5

Boyatzis, R. E. *The Competent Manager.* New York: John Wiley, 1982.

Broad, M., and J. Newstrom. *Transfer of Training.* Reading, MA: Addison-Wesley, 1992.

Caffarella, R. *Program Development and Evaluation Resource Book for Trainers.* New York: John Wiley, 1988.

Hannum, W., and C. Hansen. *Instructional Systems Development in Large Organizations.* Englewood Cliffs, NJ: Educational Technology Publications, 1989.

Kirkpatrick, D. *Techniques for Evaluating Training Programs. More Evaluating Training Programs.* Alexandria, VA: ASTD, 1987.

Kirkpatrick, D. L., and J. D. Kirkpatrick. *Evaluating Training Programs: The Four Levels* (3rd edition). San Francisco: Berrett-Koehler, 2006.

Krohnert, G. *Basic Training for Trainers* (revised edition). Sydney, Australia: McGraw-Hill Book Company, 1994.

Laird, D. *Approaches to Training and Development*. Reading, MA: Addison-Wesley, 1985.

Mager, R. *Preparing Instructional Objectives* (2nd edition). Belmont, CA: Fearon, 1975.

Marshall, V., and R. Schriver. "Using Evaluation to Improve Performance." *Technical & Skills Training*, January 1994.

McArdle, G. *Conducting a Needs Assessment*. Menlo Park, CA: Crisp Publications, 1998.

Phillips, J. J. *Handbook of Training Evaluation and Measurement Methods*. Houston: Gulf, 1991.

Phillips, J. J. *Evaluating Training Programs: The Four Levels*. San Francisco: Berrett-Koehler, 1994.

Schuler, R. S. *Human Resource Management* (5th edition). Cincinnati, OH: South Western College Publishing, 1996.

Silberman, M., and K. Lawson. *101 Ways to Make Training Active*. San Francisco: Pfeiffer, 1995.

Society for Human Resource Management Learning System Certification Guide. Alexandria, VA: Society for Human Resource Management, 1997.

Steadman, S. V. "Learning to Select a Needs Assessment Strategy." *Training and Development Journal*, January 1980.

Chapter 6

Barney, J. B., and P. M. Wright. "On Becoming a Strategic Partner: The Role of Human Resources in Gaining Competitive Advantage." *Human Resource Management*, volume 37, number 1, 1998.

Caudron, S. "Integrate HR and Training." *Workforce*, volume 77, number 5, 1998.

Dell, J., J. Fox, and R. Malcolm. "Training Situation Analysis: Conducting a Needs Analysis for Teams and New Systems." *Performance Improvement*, volume 37, number 3, 1998.

Langdon, D. G. "Selecting Interventions." *Performance Improvement*, volume 36, number 10, 1997.

Miller, C. L. "Design, Implementation, and Evaluation of a University-Industry Multimedia Presentation." *Journal of Instruction Delivery Systems*, volume 12, number 2, 1998.

Phillips, J. J., and W. J. Rothwell, editors. *Linking HRD Programs With Organizational Strategy*. Alexandria, VA: ASTD, 1998.

Shank, P. "No R-E-S-P-E-C-T? Five Foolish Things Trainers Do." *Training & Development*, volume 52, number 8, 1998.

Chapter 7

Austin, M. "Needs Assessment by Focus Group." *Infoline*, number 259401 (revised edition). Alexandria, VA: ASTD, 1998.

Brethower, D. M. "Rapid Analysis: Matching Solutions to Changing Situations." *Performance Improvement*, volume 36, number 10, 1997.

Gerson, G., and C. McCleskey. "Numbers Help Make a Training Decision That Counts." *HRMagazine*, volume 43, number 8, 1998.

Laird, D. *Approaches to Training and Development*. Reading, MA: Addison-Wesley, 1985.

Loughner, P., and L. Moller. "The Use of Task Analysis Procedures by Instructional Designers." *Performance Improvement Quarterly*, volume 11, number 3, 1998.

Ricks, D. M. "Challenging Assumptions That Block Learning." *Training*, volume 34, number 8, 1997.

Russell, S. "Training and Learning Styles." *Infoline*, number 258804 (revised edition). Alexandria, VA: ASTD, 1998.

Tampson, P. "Training Ties That Bind." *Technical Training*, volume 9, number 2, 1998.

Waagen, A. K. "Task Analysis." *Infoline*, number 259808. Alexandria, VA: ASTD, 1998.

Zemke, R. "How to Do a Needs Assessment When You Think You Don't Have Time." *Training*, volume 35, number 3, 1998.

Chapter 8

Cohen, S. L. "The Case for Custom Training." *Training & Development*, volume 52, number 8, 1998.

Coombs, S. J., and I. D. Smith. "Designing a Self-Organized Conversational Learning Environment." *Educational Technology*, volume 38, number 3, 1998.

Kules, J., and M. Smith. "Produce It or Purchase It?" *Technical & Skills Training*, volume 8, number 3, 1997.

Langdon, D. "Are Objectives Passes?" *Performance Improvement*, volume 36, number 9, 1997.

Mager, R. F. *Making Instruction Work: Or Skillbloomers*. Atlanta: Center for Effective Performance, 1997.

Moallem, M., and R. S. Earle. "Instructional Design Models and Teacher Thinking: Toward a New Conceptual Model for Research and Development." *Educational Technology*, volume 38, number 2, 1998.

Parry, S. "Organizing a Lesson Plan by Objectives." *Technical Training*, volume 9, number 4, 1998.

Plattner, F. "Instructional Objectives." *Infoline*, number 259712. Alexandria, VA: ASTD, 1997.

Chapter 9

Blanchard, P. N., and J. W. Thacker. *Effective Training: Systems, Strategies, and Practices* (2nd edition). Upper Saddle River, NJ: Prentice Hall, 2003.

Gayeski, D. M. "Out-of-the-Box Instructional Design." *Training & Development*, volume 52, number 4, 1998.

Gordon, J., and M. Hequet. "Live & in Person." *Training*, volume 34, number 3, 1997.

Reigeluth, C. M., and K. Squire. "Emerging Work on the New Paradigm of Instructional Theories." *Educational Technology*, volume 48, number 4, 1998.

Ruyle, K. E. "The 'Three R's of ROI." *Technical Training*, volume 9, number 3, 1998.

Schriver, R., and S. Giles. "Where Have All the $$$ Gone." *Technical Training*, volume 9, number 4, 1998.

Siegel, J. "How to Combine Classroom Training and Technology Delivery." *Multimedia & Internet Training Newsletter*, volume 4, number 9, 1997.

Ward, F. *Staying Legal: A Guide to Copyright and Trademark Use.* Alexandria, VA: ASTD Press, 2007.

Webb, W. "Multimedia Training on a Budget." *Training*, volume 34, number 2, 1997.

Yelon, S., and L. M. Sheppard. "Instant Lessons." *Performance Improvement*, volume 37, number 1, 1998.

Chapter 10

Chinien, C., and F. Boutin. "A Framework for Evaluating the Effectiveness of Instructional Materials." *Performance and Instruction*, volume 33, number 3, 1994.

Dick, W., and D. King. "Formative Evaluation in the Performance Context." *Performance and Instruction*, volume 33, number 9, 1994.

Duncan, J. "WBT Simulations for Safety." *Technical Training*, volume 9, number 4, 1998.

Northrup, P. T. "Concurrent Formative Evaluation: Guidelines and Implications for Multimedia Designers." *Educational Technology*, volume 35, number 6, 1995.

Provost, K. "Implementing a Web-Based Training Project." *Multimedia & Internet Training Newsletter*, volume 4, number 11, 1997.

Ramsey, B., and P. Murphy. "Human Factors Considerations in Multimedia Courseware Development." *Journal of Interactive Instruction Development*, volume 9, number 1, 1996.

Reynolds, A. "The Basics: Formative Evaluation." *Technical & Skills Training*, volume 6, number 8, 1995.

Chapter 11

Broad, M., and J. Newstrom. *Transfer of Training.* Reading, MA: Addison-Wesley, 1992.

Bureau of National Affairs. "Evaluation Evolves." *Workforce Strategies*, 16, WS-31-WS-32, June 1998.

Falletta, S. V., and W. L. Combs. "Evaluating Technical Training: A functional Approach." *Infoline*, number 259709. Alexandria, VA: ASTD, 1997.

Hale, J. "Evaluation: It's Time to Go Beyond Levels, 1, 2, 3, and 4." *Performance Improvement*, volume 37, number 2, 1998.

Kidder, P. J., and J. Z. Rouiller. "Evaluating the Success of Large-Scale Training Effort." *National Productivity Review*, volume 16, number 2, 1997.

Kirkpatrick, D. L., and J. D. Kirkpatrick. *Evaluating Training Programs: The Four Levels.* (3rd edition). San Francisco: Berrett-Koehler Publishers, 2006.

Morrow, C. C., M. Q. Jarrett, and M. T. Rupinski. "An Investigation of the Effect and Economic Utility of Corporate-wide Training." *Personnel Psychology*, volume 50, number 1, 1997.

Phillips, J. J. *Handbook of Training Evaluation and Measurement Methods.* Houston: Gulf, 1997.

Piskurich, G. M. "Reevaluating Evaluation." *Performance Improvement*, volume 36, number 8, 1997.

Robinson, D. G., and J. C. Robinson. "Measuring Affective and Behavioral Change." *Infoline*, number 259110 (revised edition). Alexandria, VA: ASTD, 1997.

Silberman, M., and K. Lawson. *101 Ways to Make Training Active.* San Francisco: Pfeiffer, 1995.

Waagen, A. K. "Essentials for Evaluation." *Infoline*, number 259705. Alexandria, VA: ASTD, 1997.

Watson, S. C. "Five Easy Pieces to Performance Measurement." *Training & Development*, volume 52, number 5, 1998.

Tool Kit

Mager, R. *Preparing Instructional Objectives* (2nd edition). Belmont, CA: Fearon, 1975.

Resources

Professional Organizations

American Society for Training & Development

ASTD is the world's largest association dedicated to workplace learning and perform-ance professionals. ASTD's members come from more than 100 countries and connect locally in 136 U.S. chapters and 25 Global Networks. Members work in thousands of organizations of all sizes, in government, as independent consultants, and suppliers.

ASTD started in 1944 when the organization held its first annual conference. ASTD has widened the profession's focus to link learning and performance to individual and organizational results, and is a sought-after voice on critical public policy issues. For more information, visit www.astd.org.

1640 King Street, Box 1443
Alexandria, VA 22313-1443
Phone: 703.683.8100
Fax: 703.683.8103
www.astd.org

International Society for Performance Improvement

ISPI is a smaller, but complementary organization to ASTD. Members join ISPI because they have an interest in instructional system development and performance improvement. Many members are instructional, curriculum, and evaluation design-ers as well as training professionals. ISPI holds an annual conference and exposition.

1400 Spring Street, Suite 260
Silver Spring, MD 20910
Phone: 301.587.8570
Fax: 301.587.8573
www.ispi.org

Toastmasters International

Toastmasters International is an organization that helps trainers as well as nontrainers to improve their communication and presentation skills. Toastmasters International has more than 8,500 clubs throughout 60 countries. The local clubs meet on a regular basis in a meeting environment that provides members the opportunity to give presentations and receive feedback on their performance from other members. Presentations that members give may be prepared in advance of the meeting or may be impromptu.

Mailing Address
P.O. Box 9052
Mission Viejo, CA 92690
Phone: 949.858.8255
http://toastmasters.org

Street Address
23182 Arroyo Vista
Rancho Santa Margarita, CA 92688

International Board of Standards for Training, Performance, and Instruction

IBSTPI's mission is to promote the definition, organization, codification, and use of the professional, disciplined craft of individual and collective performance improvement. IBSTPI consists of a board of 15 professionals that considers itself a service organization to practitioners, consumers, educators, researchers, and vendors in the training and performance improvement field. The board is responsible, in part, for the establishment and maintenance of ethical and best practice standards for professionals who serve as managers, instructional designers, or trainers in the general professional field of performance improvement for individuals and organizations. The board publishes documents, which capture and preserve the essence of the origins and history of the profession so that young professionals will have a clear image of best professional practice and ethical conduct. To date, IBSTPI has developed and disseminated competencies for instructional designers and developers, instructors, and training managers.

325 West Park Avenue
State College, PA 16803
www.ibstpi.org

Magazines and Journals

T+D

This magazine is for the training and HRD practitioner, published monthly by ASTD.

Training

This journal is for the training practitioner, published monthly by Lakewood Publications.

50 South Ninth Street
Minneapolis, MN 55402
Phone: 612.233.0471.

PI

This resource is for the trainer and instructional designer, published monthly except for combined May/June and November/December issues by ISPI.

Trainer Certification Resources

Certificate In Training offers online course modules and faculty mentoring for each participant and is sponsored by the Florida Gulf Coast University, Center for Technology and Innovation. The initial course will certify you as an instructional designer. You will be assigned a faculty mentor and will complete a capstone project that will be reviewed by the faculty that supports your candidacy.

Phone: 239.590.1000
www.fgcu.edu

About the Author

Geri McArdle has been a practitioner in the human resource field for 20 years and has published nine books on human productivity and numerous research journal articles in the area of human resource development and training. She has served as the coordinator of a PhD program in human resource development at Barry University in Fort Myers, Florida, for the past four years and is one of the ASTD seven master trainers recognized by *T+D*. She obtained her PhD from Syracuse University and is a Harvard University postdoctoral fellow at the Philosophy of Education Research Center.